THE POLITICAL CHRIST

THE
POLITICAL
CHRIST

ALAN RICHARDSON

THE WESTMINSTER PRESS
PHILADELPHIA

COPYRIGHT © SCM PRESS LTD 1973

PUBLISHED BY THE WESTMINSTER PRESS ®
PHILADELPHIA, PENNSYLVANIA

PRINTED IN THE UNITED STATES OF AMERICA

Library of Congress Cataloging in Publication Data

Richardson, Alan, 1905–
   The political Christ.

    1.   Christianity and politics—History.
2.   Jesus Christ—Person and offices. I. Title.
BR115.P7R485   232   73-14598
ISBN 0-664-20986-6

CONTENTS

I   The Political Environment of the Ministry of Jesus   1

II The Political Involvement of Jesus   28

III The Attitude of the Early Church to Political Authority   53

IV The Political Christ in History and Today   86

    Notes   113

I

THE POLITICAL ENVIRONMENT OF THE MINISTRY OF JESUS

One thing which may be asserted with confidence is that from its earliest beginnings Christian faith has consistently affirmed the real humanity of Jesus Christ. In whatever respects he may have differed from other men, he shared with them the temptations, sufferings and death which are the common lot. The phrase in the Apostles' Creed 'suffered under Pontius Pilate' involves total commitment to the belief that he lived a truly human life at an identifiable moment in public history.[1] As Paul reminded Festus some thirty years after Jesus' execution by one of his own predecessors in office, 'these things were not done in a corner' (Acts 26.26). The circumstances of Christ's life and death and of the rise of the Christian Church must therefore be accessible to the inspection of historians. Amongst these circumstances must be (at least in principle) the whole political situation in which Jesus' life was set and his attitude towards it. If, therefore, we wish to consider seriously the political implications of the life, teaching and death of Christ, we must begin by considering the political configuration of the place of his upbringing, from which he never travelled more than sixty or seventy miles in his life.

THE HERODS

Jesus was born towards the end of the reign of King Herod, who died in 4 BC. Herod is one of that select company upon whom Clio, a capricious Muse, has conferred the title 'the Great' (along with Alexander, Constantine, Charlemagne, Peter and Frederick). If, as Lord Acton said, great men are almost always bad men, Herod

1

was well qualified for the distinction. His father, Antipater, was an Idumean (Greek for Edomite), that is, a member of a southern non-Jewish tribe which had been forcibly converted to Judaism by John Hyrcanus in 109 BC. He had been appointed by Julius Caesar as administrator of Judea in 47 BC, when the high-priestly Hasmonean house was proving incompetent to govern the turbulent and faction-ridden populace. After his father's death (43 BC) Herod had to flee the country, and in Rome he won the favour of Mark Antony and subsequently of Caesar Augustus. The Romans were not yet ready to take direct responsibility for the administration of Judea, though they knew it to be a vital link in the line of communications in their eastern territories. A friendly client-king was just what they needed. They conferred upon Herod the title 'King of Judea', which meant nothing more than permission to conquer a kingdom if he could (40 BC). With a small company of personal followers, but without Roman military assistance, he landed on the shore of Palestine and by 37 BC he had set up his kingdom in Jerusalem.

Herod at once devoted his energies to the task of ruthlessly eliminating every possible rival upon whom his paranoiac suspicions fell. His reign, says Cecil Roth, though undisturbed by foreign war, was stained with cruelties and atrocities of a character almost without a parallel in history. The Hasmonean family was virtually wiped out. The brigands, who in a time of economic distress infested the mountains which had once been regarded as the bulwarks of the Holy City's safety (Pss. 121.1; 125.2), were reduced to impotence. Ordinary folk, shopkeepers and peasants, had good reason to be grateful to Herod; for as has been well said, he made life and property in Judea safe from every tyranny except his own. He had restored something of its former prestige to the Jewish nation, and in order to conciliate the people he had prudently married Mariamne, a granddaughter of John Hyrcanus, the last legal Hasmonean ruler. But the Jews were not reconciled. They knew that Herod wore his Judaism like a cloak, to be discarded when he attended the Greek festivals and games in honour of the pagan gods while visiting foreign cities, where he also erected costly buildings with Jewish money. Like so many rulers before and after him, Herod had a passion for architecture. His rebuilding of the Temple in Jerusalem (John 2.20), doubtless intended to please his subjects, caused great offence: by what right did this Idumean half-Jew lay hands upon their Holy

Place? Herod's way of life outraged the ethical susceptibilities of the non-permissive Jewish society. He had married ten wives and had fourteen children. As was usual in oriental despotisms, when Herod was growing old, his sons by different wives vied with one another for the succession. Fearing that one of them might assassinate him, Herod disposed of them, as formerly he had ruthlessly eliminated all possible rivals. (Mariamne had been put to death: her two sons, being descended from the old royal line, would be especially dangerous.) Augustus in Rome, watching the scene with cynical amusement, is credited with a pun in Greek which has been rendered in English as 'I would rather be Herod's sow than Herod's son.' The story of the massacre of the innocents (Matt. 2.13-18) is historically important in the sense that it witnesses to the deep impression of Herod's cruelty which survived in the popular memory for a century after his death: he would slay a thousand infants if he suspected that one of them might become a rival King of the Jews.

On Herod's death in 4 BC the considerable territory over which he ruled was divided among his surviving sons. Archelaus received the title of King of Judea (cf. Matt. 2.22), but he was too weak to maintain the law and order which the Romans required; they deposed him in AD 6, bringing Judea for the first time under direct Roman rule. Philip was made Tetrarch of Iturea, a vaguely defined area well to the East of the Jordan. (The word 'tetrarch' had come to mean 'princeling', the local ruler of a part of a wider political whole, having lost its literal meaning of 'a ruler of a fourth part'.) Another son, Herod Antipas, the Herod of the gospels, was made Tetrarch of Galilee and Perea (the region immediately eastwards beyond the Jordan; Matt. 19.1; John 10.40). He posed as a Jew amongst his Jewish subjects, but did not gain their respect. His mother was a Samaritan, one of the foreign women whom Herod the Great had married. His first wife was the daughter of the Arabian King Aretas; he put her away in order to marry Herodias, the wife of his half-brother, Herod Philip (not the Philip mentioned above). It was this marriage which John the Baptist denounced, since it was incestuous according to Jewish law. Herod's consequent execution of the Baptist shows that he cared little for Jewish law or for Jewish opinion, which held John to be a prophet (Mark 11.32). The colourful story in Mark 6.14-19 is historically interesting as indicating how Herod's crime of vengeance had entered into Jewish folk-lore as recounted forty years after the event; its embroideries testify to

3

the popular assessment of Herod's character. It is unlikely that the princess Salome would have taken the part of a dancing slave-girl (a commodity not in short supply in the palaces of the Herods) at a banquet given by her father for his petty officials. The story, as Mark tells it, belongs to the mythology of the early Church, which saw in the encounter of John with Herod and Herodias a re-enactment of the struggle of Elijah with Ahab and Jezebel (I Kings 17-22), but this time it was the Elijah *redivivus* who perished (Mark 9.11-13; Matt. 11.14). Whether Herodias exercised an evil influence comparable to that of Jezebel may be doubted, but her ambition brought about the downfall of Antipas. She persuaded him to go to Rome and supplicate to be made king. (The expression 'King Herod' in Mark 6.14 is only a courtesy title and is corrected in Matt. 14.1.) The Romans, however, banished him to Gaul (AD 39), where he died. His nephew, Herod Agrippa I, had been successfully intriguing against him.

The gospel writers supply some interesting information concerning the attitudes of Herod and Jesus towards each other. But they do so only incidentally, because they were not at all interested in our modern concern about Jesus' involvement in the politics of his day. They mention, for instance, 'the Herodians' (Matt. 22.16; Mark 3.6; 12.13) who joined with the Pharisees, who otherwise would have had nothing in common with them, to ensnare Jesus in argument. We know nothing about a pro-Herod party from any other source, but presumably Herod must have had some political supporters or hangers-on. Herod himself was curious about Jesus, as a result of the reports he had heard. Like others who have no religious belief, he was highly superstitious; at one time he wondered whether John the Baptist had risen from the dead, as some people were saying (Luke 9.7-9; cf. Mark 8.28). He had long been anxious to meet Jesus and perhaps to see him perform one of the marvellous works with which he was credited; he was gratified when Pilate, hitherto so unfriendly, gave him the opportunity, but he must have been disappointed by Jesus' refusal to respond (Luke 23.7-12). Jesus for his part deliberately avoided Herod, whom he shrewdly recognized as one who ruled by craft rather than by strength. His reference to Herod as 'that fox' must surely be reckoned among the authentic words of Jesus; it sums up the verdict of history. He outwitted Herod and his minions, as he had to do if he was to fulfil his mission in Jerusalem (Luke 13.31-33). On his final journey to the Holy City he avoided Herod's attentions by travelling through Samaria, where as a pilgrim going up to the festival he was unwelcome (Luke 9.51-53): it was not fitting that a prophet should perish outside Jerusalem as the Baptist had done. The gospel writers were not historians, aiming to give a factual record of events in orderly sequence; nevertheless, whatever the literary critics may say, by depicting Jesus as a real man caught up in an actual political situation, they bring us into touch with the very stuff of history, the raw material upon which the historian today can and must go to work with all the tools of his trade.

Herod Agrippa I was the grandson of Herod the Great and Mariamne; his father, Aristobulus, had been put to death by Herod when Agrippa was four years old (6 BC). Much of his youth had been spent in Rome, where in spite of the disapproval of the Emperor Tiberius, he became a court favourite and a friend of Gaius Caligula. When Tiberius died, Caligula succeeded him (37 BC), but in the year that the Senate conferred upon him the imperial power he had a serious illness which left him mentally unbalanced (everyone knows about his wish to make his horse a consul); he became vain and overbearing. Agrippa was given tetrarchies in Palestine, and in AD 41 he received the title of king. His mettle was soon put to the test, for in that year he had the courage to resist his patron, whose vengeance on those who opposed him was terrible. Oriental ideas about the divinity of the ruler had now spread into the West, and Caligula was the first Roman Emperor to take his divine status seriously. He ordered a statue of himself to be placed in the Temple at Jerusalem. Agrippa risked all that he had gained by intervening to dissuade Caligula from enforcing his decree. He thus served his Jewish subjects well by averting the tumult and the bloody reprisals which would inevitably have resulted from the profanation of the Temple by such a transgression of the first two commandments of the Decalogue (Ex. 20.2-6). With his Jewish subjects Agrippa enjoyed a brief but ecstatic honeymoon: he ruled over a kingdom broader even than that of his grandfather, and he had restored the national pride of the Jews. They seemed to themselves to be an independent state once more, for there was no longer a Roman procurator over them. Indeed, Agrippa's short reign has been described as the Indian summer of Judaism. Seeing that it pleased the Jews, he persecuted the Christian 'sect'; he executed the apostle James, the brother of John, and put Peter in prison (Acts 12.1-19). But the Herodian leopard had not changed his spots; amongst his Gentile subjects he cast aside his Jewish cloak. One day in AD 44 in Caesarea, when he was parading himself as a god and receiving the adulation of the multitudes, he was struck down by a fatal disease ('eaten of worms', whatever that may mean) while making an oration (Acts 12.22f.). The last king of the Jews was dead. The Jews as well as the Christians regarded his fate as a divine punishment for his impiety.

When Agrippa died, his son, known as Herod Agrippa II, was a lad of seventeen, and his father's kingdom became a Roman province once more. In AD 53 the young Agrippa returned to Palestine and received some of his father's possessions, which enabled him to indulge the Herodian passion for architecture. But he never exercised political authority and was never popular with the Jews. The Romans regarded him as their adviser on Jewish affairs in Palestine, as in the case of Paul's examination before Festus the Procurator (Acts 25.13–26.32; the reference to 'Agrippa the King' in 25.13 is only a courtesy title). He had the oversight of the Temple and was credited with being 'expert in all Jewish customs and questions' (Acts 26.3). He tried desperately to prevent the outbreak of the Jewish rebellion against Rome, which started in AD 66. His sister Bernice, who was present with him at Paul's examination, is also credited with heroic efforts to prevent the massacre of the revolting Jews by the Procurator Florus; but both she and her younger sister Drusilla (the wife of Felix, Acts 24.24) gained a reputation as ladies of doubtful virtue. After the outbreak of the war Agrippa and his sisters withdrew to Rome, where Bernice continued to be the mistress of Titus, the destroyer of Jerusalem in AD 70, who became Emperor in AD 79. Agrippa, the last of the Herods, attended the celebrations in Rome after the fall of Jerusalem. He died there about AD 100.

THE PROCURATORS

After the deposition of Archelaus in AD 6 Judea was placed under direct Roman rule. From that date until the outbreak of the Jewish War in AD 66 the Province was governed by procurators with the exception of the years when Herod Agrippa was king (41-44). The names of all fourteen procurators during these six decades are known to us, but only five of them require mention for our purpose. A procurator was originally a steward or bailiff who looked after his master's affairs, collecting his dues and so on. If he were the steward of a great magnate, he would exercise delegated responsibility for the government of a considerable area. Thus, Caesar's procurators were in fact the rulers of the less important provinces, although the Governor of a more important and larger province might keep an eye on his activities – as Syria seems to have exercised some oversight in Judea. The procurators were usually of equestrian rank in Roman society, like the 'most excellent' Theophilus (Luke 1.3) to whom Luke's Gospel and Acts were addressed. They were usually appointed as rulers of transitional provinces which were as yet only in process of being incorporated into the Empire, in fact, provinces like Judea after AD 6. Thus, though the Procurator of Judea was accountable to Caesar and in a loose kind of way to the Governor of Syria, he was the virtual political authority over the province, holding full financial, administrative and judicial power, including the power of life and death, and commanding all the troops stationed within his jurisdiction. The only appeal against his verdict was an appeal to Caesar himself. Too many complaints to Caesar against his administration might lead to his deposition; but, so long as he remained in office, he was in his province the embodiment and agent of the imperial power.

A fascinating treatise could be written on the word 'imperial' (from the Latin *imperialis*, pertaining to the *imperium*, supreme command, empire; cf. *impero*, to command). 'Imperial' and its pejorative derivative 'imperialist' in today's climate of opinion are widely used in connection with the British (and American) democratic systems, but curiously enough are rarely applied to the monolithic Russian *imperium*, which much more nearly resembles the Roman model, if one leaves out of account the Roman concern for equal law and even-handed justice. The Romans were interested in keeping the peace (the famous *pax Romana*) and they were politically shrewd enough to perceive that over their vast *imperium* they could achieve this only if a majority of the people in a province could be brought to realize that they could live their own lives more happily when freed from the wars and impositions of the local tyrants, the ravages of brigands and the threat of foreign invasion. An equitable administration of public law (even though legal systems are always weighted in favour of those who enforce them) is a priceless boon to ordinary folk in every age, and, when it was established as widely as was the Roman *imperium*, it offered opportunities of participation in the vast common market of the whole Mediterranean world. However, as might have been expected, the Jews would prove hard to convince. Their law said that they should not put a foreigner to reign over them (Deut. 17.15), and even the circumcised Herods were regarded as at best only half-Jews. It was in fact their religion which rendered the Jews indigestible and which precipitated the catastrophe of AD 70. The dice were loaded against the procurators from the start.

Each of the ancient empires contributed something to the development of civilization. After the conquests of Alexander the Great (d. 322 BC) the Greeks conducted a cultural mission, carrying their ideal of *paideia* (humane education, art, philosophy and free enquiry) into the world, leaving not even Jewish thought untouched. Above all, they left behind their vanished empire a *lingua franca*, spoken by all whose business carried them beyond their native land; even in the time of St Paul more Greek was spoken in cosmopolitan Rome than Latin. (It was probably there that Mark of Jerusalem wrote his gospel – in Greek – about the time of the outbreak of the Jewish War.) The Romans were not purveyors of culture. They were practical men, organizers, surveyors, engineers, road-makers, administrators and soldiers; the late Mr Christopher Dawson somewhat unkindly said that the Roman achievement could be summed up in the sentence, 'Balbus built a wall'.[2] But he also added that they 'served the cause of Western culture better than the spectacular achievements of Alexander and his successors'. Above all, they established the concept of law in the region which was later called Europe; in their Asian provinces such success as they obtained was not lasting. They were realists, not idealists with a civilizing mission. They imposed taxes upon the peoples they subdued; they so arranged matters that the wealth of the Orient and the corn of Egypt flowed into the Tiber; and, since it was necessary to put down rivals as well as brigands on the land and pirates on the sea, they deployed well-disciplined forces to keep the peace from the Rhine and Danube to the Sahara, and from Hadrian's Wall to the Black Sea and the Orontes. They conferred the blessings of strong and orderly government upon their subject peoples, but they were not a welfare state. They did not build schools, universities and hospitals, nor did they provide social services for the aged and the poor. The Roman Empire

did not eventually dismantle itself in the process of bringing its
dependencies to the point at which they were ready to govern themselves. Its collapse left the provinces at the mercy of the barbarian
invaders in the West and (at a later date) of the hordes of Islam
in Africa and the East.

Pontius Pilatus took up his appointment as Procurator of Judea
in AD 26. It is unfortunate for the reputation of the Romans that
his is the name which has been more widely known down the
centuries than that of any emperor. On the whole the governors of
the provinces were able and conscientious administrators; but Judea
was a far-away outpost of empire and appointment there might
be regarded as banishment – which indeed such appointments sometimes actually were in the case of those who had fallen into dis-
favour. From his arrival Pilate despised the natives with all the
arrogance of an aristocratic colonial governor far from home. (His
racialist prejudice is skilfully depicted in his scornful outburst
'Am I a Jew?' in John 18.35, where the author of the gospel conveys
the truth of history, as he understood it, in the words which he
puts into the mouths of Jesus and Pilate: there were, of course, no
reporters present whose verbatim accounts have survived.) On his
arrival Pilate withdrew the concession granted by his predecessors
that the images of the Emperor on the army's standards should be
removed before they entered the gates of the Holy City; they were
offensive to the Jews because they symbolized the rule of a foreigner
and also contravened the Second Commandment. When his threat
of the death penalty failed to move the protesters who had travelled
to his government headquarters at Caesarea and who passively
awaited their execution, he found himself forced to order the
removal of the images. Another offence against Jewish susceptibilities was his raiding of the Temple treasury for money (which
had been given to God) with which to build aqueducts for bringing
more water into Jerusalem, in itself a much-needed commodity
especially during the feasts. One atrocity of which we otherwise
know nothing is mentioned during the course of Jesus' ministry
as a happening well known to his hearers: Pilate's slaughter of
certain Galilean pilgrims who had gone up to Jerusalem to offer
sacrifice at the feast (Luke 13.1-4). Though the passage is found
only in Luke's Gospel, it must have been derived from an authentic
tradition; Luke with his interest in commending the gospel of
Christ to the Roman ruling class would hardly have been likely to

have invented it himself, since it showed the Procurator in an unfavourable light. It is of importance in the contemporary discussion about whether Jesus favoured revolutionary action against the Roman occupation. Jesus does not use the incident to make revolutionary propaganda but to correct the popular false theory about suffering: victims of disasters, such as capricious deeds of violence or the collapse of the tower at Siloam, were not to be regarded as having received divine retribution for some concealed hideous sinfulness.

We must reserve for the present the question of Pilate's role in the story of the trial of Jesus. That he condemned Jesus to death is indisputable; the circumstances in which he did so have been the subject of a long and complicated debate amongst scholars. His decision, which has secured for Pilate a permanent place in world history, did not become a ground for complaint against him at Caesar's court; influential friends were needed to gain access to that tribunal. Four of the sons of Herod Agrippa, together with certain leading Jews, once successfully petitioned Tiberius Caesar to order Pilate to remove certain offensive commemorative shields which he had set up in Herod's palace in Jerusalem;[3] Pilate seems to have used this palace as his headquarters when he came up to Jerusalem from Caesarea to keep order at the crowded feasts. (He had permanently commandeered Herod's palace in Caesarea for his own use as the Government House.) Doubtless Pilate was apprehensive not only about the complaints of leading Jews concerning his misrule but also about those of the Herods, towards whom his attitude was supercilious. It may well be that Pilate, when Jesus was brought before his judgment-seat, was taking the opportunity of conciliating both Herod and the Jewish leaders, even though he personally considered that Jesus was not in fact a revolutionary (Mark 15.14; Luke 23.4, etc.). This is certainly what the gospels suggest, but we have still to enquire whether their evidence is reliable on this vital point. Certainly Pilate was in no position to risk a charge of not being Caesar's friend; John brings out the irony of the situation with his usual skill, whether the words are put by him into the mouth of the accusers or belong to an older tradition: John 19.12; cf. Luke 23.2. According to all the evangelists, the Procurator was manoeuvered into the absurd position of condemning one whom he did not consider to be a violent revolutionary and releasing from prison one whom everyone knew to have committed insurrection with violence, while those who were accusing him of not being Caesar's friend were calling for the setting free of the notorious and violent revolutionary leader, Barabbas. The clever Jewish accusers of Jesus, having no use for one who challenged their authority, outwitted the slow-moving official mind by pretending to be concerned for Caesar's goodwill and thus securing the release of a convicted revolutionary who was a popular idol of the nationalistic Jews.

Pilate continued in office until AD 36, when Vitellius, the Legate in Syria, ordered him to go to Rome to answer charges of misgovernment. The immediate complaint against him was his massacre of some harmless Samaritans who had responded to the call of an impostor promising to show them the treasure hidden by Moses near their sacred mountain, Gerizim. Tiberius died before Pilate reached Rome, but he seems to have been banished to South Gaul, where he disappeared from history but not from legend.[4] Judea continued to be governed by procurators, apart from the brief interlude of the reign of Herod Agrippa I (41-44), until the outbreak of the Jewish War in 66. The two procurators who figure in the Acts of the Apostles, Antonius Felix (52-58) and Porcius Festus (58-61) were relatively good rulers in comparison with their successors. Even so, we read that the 'most excellent' (Acts 23.26; 24.3) Felix dallied in the matter of Paul's trial and kept him in custody, hoping for a bribe (24.26), and when he did not receive it, left him in prison for two years in Caesarea, desiring to gain favour with the Jews (24.27). Festus was the best of the procurators in the whole of this period; he had to deal with the case which Felix had left on his hands. But he also wished to please the Jews, and his suggestion that Paul should stand trial in Jerusalem provoked Paul to exercise his right as a Roman citizen to appeal to Caesar in Rome (Acts 25.9-12). After the short period of Festus in office the antagonism which led to the destruction of Jerusalem was inevitable, given the callousness of the Romans and the intransigence of the Jews. The misrule of such cruel procurators as Albinus (61-65) and Gessius Florus (65-66), the last of the line, finally provoked the mass of the people, including many of the religious leaders, to make common cause with the nationalist guerillas whose numbers had greatly increased, and the Jewish War, as it was called by the Romans, began.

There were in the days of the procurators three principal Jewish parties (*haireseis*, sects, e.g. Acts 26.5). This is the word from which our English 'heresy' is derived, and it meant the party or opinion which one has chosen for oneself. Paul even speaks of 'the Christian heresy' (Acts 28.22), which reminds us that Christianity began life as a sect within Judaism; the word had not acquired the pejorative overtones which can be detected in Paul's condemnation of the party strife which broke out in the church of Corinth (I Cor. 11.18f.; cf. 1.10; 12.25). The Jewish sects were not nonconformist; their members all worshipped together in the Temple. To be a Jew meant to belong to a people rather than to give assent to a precisely defined doctrinal definition or to hold a common political opinion. The Jews were tolerant amongst themselves and did not excommunicate one another, but they excluded all non-Jews, and even would-be Jews such as the Samaritans, with whom they would have no dealings (John 4.9).

The three principal sects were the Sadducees, the Pharisees and the Essenes. Of these only the Sadducees were a political party. The Pharisees had no political ambitions or indeed interest. They regarded the Roman occupation as a divine punishment for their nation's failure to live according to the Torah (Law of Moses) as elaborated by their oral tradition: God would in his own good time remove the foreign overlords when the Jews faithfully observed his commandments, or even (according to one rabbi) when only one Jew kept the Law perfectly for only one day. The Essenes were an ascetic monastic-type brotherhood who had opted out of society altogether, and for this reason it is unnecessary for us to discuss them further. Smaller sects, like that of the Baptists, the adherents of John the Baptist, originating in the days of Jesus himself but continuing in existence for several centuries (cf. Acts 19.1-7), likewise have little relevance for our purpose. In what sense, if any, the Zealots can be said to have existed as a coherent political party in the time of Jesus is an open question which we must examine later.

The Sadducees and the Sanhedrin

The Sadducees constituted an hereditary aristocracy of (it is said) about two hundred families from which the high priests were drawn. They traced their descent from Zadok, whom King Solomon had appointed High Priest (I Kings 2.26ff.) and who in his turn traced his descent from Aaron. The Pharisees never questioned the legitimacy of the Sadducean high priesthood. After the decline of the Hasmonean dynasty the Sadducees held a position of considerable prominence, but Pompey on his visit to Jerusalem (63 BC) and King Herod at a later date (37 BC) deemed it expedient to diminish their numbers by a series of executions. Herod also appointed and removed high priests at will and diluted their influence by filling the Sanhedrin (the High Court of Justice) with his own nominees, thus enlarging the aristocracy with new high priestly families. The Sanhedrin was kept in being by the Romans and was entrusted by them with the control of internal Jewish affairs; it was a convenient means of giving the populace the illusion of self-government. The Sadducees for their part were willing to serve in the puppet government which the Sanhedrin had now become, because they well knew that they were dependent on the Romans for the continuance of their privileged position in the country. The High Priest was the president of the Sanhedrin, which in theory consisted of seventy members (presbyters, elders) on the model of Moses' council (Num. 11.16). It is not entirely clear how appointments to the Sanhedrin were made, and certainly some learned and distinguished Pharisees were members of it (e.g. Gamaliel, Acts 5.34). Most of the members were, however, Sadducees whose fortune it was to have been born into the right family. One qualified for membership of the party by birth; one could hardly choose to become a Sadducee; one could only decide to be a hanger-on.

Naturally the Sadducees were conservatives. They did not want to alter the *status quo*; from their point of view any change would be a change for the worse. They were not the real rulers of the country but they could pretend that they were at the price of deferring to the Romans in all important matters. Since they controlled the Temple, the Sadducees had control also of the treasury, to which the hordes of pilgrims and the poorest widows (cf. Mark

12.41-44) devoutly made their contribution. They did a lucrative trade in exchanging at profitable rates the pilgrims' money into the Temple currency with which alone travellers from afar could buy the animals and doves which they wanted to offer in sacrifice. This, after all, was the object of their journey, and it was hardly practical to bring their own animal victims from (say) Pontus and Asia, Phrygia and Pamphylia, Egypt and the parts of Libya about Cyrene. Jesus did not have to be a fanatical national revolutionary to find this exploitation of the pilgrims highly offensive, the making of the house of God into a den of lēstai – the very word in common use to denote the brigands, maurauding bands and revolutionary guerillas: Jesus declared that the high priests and their agents were the real robbers! (cf. Mark 11.15-18).

The Sadducees were conservative in doctrine as well as in politics. The newfangled beliefs of the Pharisees were not favoured: the resurrection of the dead (both of soul and body), angels and spirits, a Messiah who would level the scores with the Romans – such novelties were dangerous. The old Book (the Torah, i.e. Pentateuch) was good enough for them. Not that they actually rejected the Prophets and the Writings: they might be read for example of life and instruction of manners, but they should not be applied to establish any doctrine. The fact is that the Sadducees were not religious men. They were worldly members of an aristocracy which was at ease in Zion, having made their compromise with the Romans (cf. John 11.48). The high priests doubtless carried out their traditional functions as to the manner born, as indeed they were, but they had no sympathy with the Pharisaic insistence upon carrying their scribal elaboration of the Law into ordinary daily life. They were accustomed by their breeding to rubbing shoulders and even sitting down to dine with foreign princes and notables, habits which the Pharisees would have regarded as defilement. The Sadducees naturally supported the establishment, and the established religion was both the adornment and bulwark of the *status quo*. Since they constituted the majority party in the Sanhedrin, the most damning charge which could be levelled against Jesus when he was brought before that body would be that he had threatened to destroy the Temple (Mark 14.58): was it not he who had denounced their profitable commercial enterprise there? Such a charge would be enough to secure his condemnation, though it apparently proved necessary, because of the confusion of the witnesses, to bring in a further charge of blasphemy (Mark 14.55-64; the word translated as 'council' in RV and NEB is in the Greek text *synedrion*, Sanhedrin).

But the Sanhedrin was by no means an homogeneous body. The gospels record that two members, at least, were sympathizers with Jesus and were in fact secretly his disciples. Mark implies (15.43) and Matthew states (27.57) that Joseph of Arimathea was a disciple; John 19.38 also says that he was a secret disciple; Luke 23.51 adds that he had not consented to the verdict of condemnation which had been passed at the examination before the Sanhedrin. Joseph had begged and obtained Pilate's permission to bury the body of Jesus, doubtless for a consideration, since every procurator had his price. John (3.1ff.), who alone mentions Nicodemus, tells us that he was 'a ruler of the Jews' (i.e. a member of the Sanhedrin) and a Pharisee, and that he was also a secret disciple; he assisted Joseph at the burial in the garden tomb (19.39). Whatever one may think about John's apparent custom of bringing out the truth of history by means of scenes and speeches of his own composition, his evidence that there was sympathy for Jesus amongst Pharisaic members of the Sanhedrin is not to be lightly dismissed, since it is generally conceded nowadays that John, whoever he was, knew the Jewish *mise en scène* very well and was not (as used to be suggested) merely a Greek tourist in Palestine in search of local colour. But here, as in so many places, we are on uncertain ground. It could, for example, be argued that, if Joseph was a Pharisee, like Nicodemus, he was only fulfilling a work of piety held in high regard in devout Jewish circles, and that for this deed of charity the Christian tradition has conferred on Joseph and Nicodemus the status of discipleship. Alternatively there is the view of those literary critics who are professionally committed to the theory that the gospels are not historical documents that Joseph was introduced into the gospel tradition in the first instance as a typological fulfilment of Old Testament prophecy: as the patriarch Joseph had sought leave from Pharaoh to bury the body of Jacob (the original 'Israel': Gen. 50.4-13), so now another Joseph begs leave from the governor to bury the body of the New Israel. Of course, fulfilments of Old Testament types are found in the New Testament, but this suggestion seems particularly far-fetched; and, of course, there is the difficulty that it leaves 'of Arimathea' unexplained. The mention of a particular place (Luke calls it 'a city of the Jews,

23.51) seems to imply a definite identification with a real person who was known to the earliest Christian community. The varying traditions (they are not reports of modern-style journalists who attend trials in a professional capacity) of the examination of Jesus before the Sanhedrin, Herod and Pilate are tantalizingly brief and at points are mutually inconsistent, so that it is inevitable that scholars should vary widely in their interpretation of the evidence. It is hardly surprising that the author of one of the latest books[5] on the subject has decided to ignore their help altogether and to go it alone. But this is like putting out our feeble torches and groping along in the darkness because we do not have a searchlight.

THE PHARISEES

The Pharisees were professedly religious men and did not concern themselves with politics, except when their most cherished convictions were outraged. For instance, when in 4 BC King Herod set up a golden eagle over the chief entrance to the Temple, they struck it down; Herod, doubtless fearing that his Roman patrons would regard this essentially religious reaction as a symptom of political insubordination, ordered several of the Pharisees to be burnt alive. But in more normal times the Pharisees adhered to the doctrine that a nation gets the government it deserves:[6] the Romans were the instrument of divine chastisement of God's people for their failure to keep his commandments. In later Judaism devotion to the Law (Torah) became a warm and deeply moving expression of the individual's love of God (read, e.g., Ps. 119). Such personal holiness was doubtless not lacking amongst many Pharisees in the days of Jesus; but when religion becomes fashionable, its observances often become outward signs of social respectability and sincerity departs. In other lands and other centuries the phenomenon has reappeared: Victorian England could provide a parallel. But it would obviously be wrong to suppose that in the Victorian era there were no humble and sincere believers, and it may be presumed that in the Judea of the procurators there were those who trusted in God rather than in their own meritorious conduct. Even so, the fundamental opposition between Pharisaic orthodoxy and the teaching of Jesus must not be minimized; they radically disagreed about the character of God and his dealings

16

with mankind. But the disagreement had nothing to do with the political situation in Palestine, even though in the end the Pharisees joined with the politically-oriented Sadducees and Herodians (Mark 3.6) to do away with Jesus.

Jesus charged the Pharisees with insincerity. The word he used of them (in Aramaic) is translated in the gospels by 'hypocrites' (e.g. Matt. 6.2), a Greek word which in one of its meanings signifies actors in a stage play. An actor assumes a role which is not his character in real life; this is his profession. The derivative meaning is thus 'one who pretends to be what he is not', that is (in our normal English usage) a hypocrite. Thus in Mark 12.40 the scribes (sc. of the Pharisees), the legally trained officials, devour widows' houses even while for a pretence they make long prayers. Hypocrites blow their trumpet when they give alms, so that everyone will notice; they pray at the street corners where everyone will see them – and that is all the reward they will get (Matt. 6.2-5). Their boasted contributions to the moral assets of Judaism were paid in counterfeit coin.[7] Nevertheless Christians who have long been familiar with the gospel strictures on the Pharisees need always to remind themselves that it is easy to acquire a drugged conscience by adopting a pharisaical attitude towards the Pharisees and thanking God that they are not like them: they do not fast twice a week or give a tenth of all that they get to their church or to Christian Aid. The Pharisees at least set high standards for themselves, and some of them must have reached levels of disciplined living and giving which could not have been attained if they had set their targets lower. Christians are by no means exempt from indulgence in self-congratulation at their attainment of the minimum demands of conventional religious respectability. In the parable of Jesus it was the penitent tax-collector, an outcast from the synagogues of the religious folk, who went home from the Temple justified in God's sight rather than the Pharisee who had many virtuous deeds of which he could boast (Luke 18.9-14). Those who are acceptable to the all-holy God are those who acknowledge that, when judged by the standards of the absolute law of love, even after they have done all that the law requires of them, they are unprofitable servants still (Luke 17.7-10). This is a religious insight, not a political one, but it has far-reaching implications both for those engaged in politics and for those who (like the Pharisees) are content to leave politics alone. Christians who today live under a democratic form of government, if they decline to have anything to do with politics on the grounds that 'politics is a dirty business', are pretending to avoid defilement by opting out of a responsibility which the Pharisees, living under the rule of the procurators, did not have.

The Pharisaic political ideal was an Israel over which God would reign in the person of his Messiah, who would be a descendant of David (cf. Mark 12.35) but not a divine figure. He would restore the kingdom to Israel, when at last Israel was worthy of the blessings of the messianic age through her obedience to the Law. Hence they set to work to codify the 639 precepts of the Torah (the first five Old Testament books, all attributed to Moses) and to make them applicable to every conceivable circumstance of daily life. This process had been going on for many years before the birth of Jesus and the result was a vast elaboration of oral interpretation handed down by different schools of 'rabbis' (masters, teachers, doctors) to their disciples who in turn added their own glosses and handed them on to their own pupils, and so on. This corpus of oral legislation is called 'the tradition of the elders' in Mark 7.3. There was broad agreement amongst the various schools of interpretation, but there were also marked differences of emphasis. Thus, the school of the learned, modest and gentle Hillel (c. 60 BC – c. AD 10) favoured a less rigorous interpretation of the Law than that of his contemporary Shammai, who advocated strictness; there was considerable rivalry between the two schools. But all the Pharisaic schools were unanimous in condemning the new Galilean preacher whom men called 'rabbi' (literally 'my master'), a term of respect used in greeting a teacher or learned man, but not necessarily implying official authorization or ordination. Though he himself was addressed by his own disciples as 'rabbi' (Mark 9.5; 11.21, etc.), he is recorded as bidding his disciples to reject the title (Matt. 21.8). John the Baptist is addressed by his disciples as 'rabbi' in John 3.26. 'Rabboni' (Mark 10.51; John 20.16) is the transliteration of an Aramaic form of the word and is an equivalent of 'rabbi'.

How Jesus acquired the knowledge of the Law which he obviously possessed and which is attested by the application to him of the title 'rabbi' remains something of a problem. It is hardly conceivable that he had belonged to any school of the Pharisees; but his understanding of the scriptures seems deeper and more comprehensive than could have been attainable through attendance at the sabbath school of the village rabbi at Nazareth. Yet at the very outset of his public ministry we find him teaching in the synagogue at Capernaum on the sabbath day, as though he were an accredited rabbi (Mark 1.21-27). But the difference between his style and that of the trained scribes is already evident: he taught as one who possessed personal authority, quite differently from the scribes, who always quoted other scribes as their authorities. One explanation, favoured by an influential group of scholars today, might be that what Jesus actually said and taught is largely irrecoverable by us, because what we find in the gospels is the tradition of the early Christian community in controversy with its Jewish opponents. The disputations between the Church and the Synagogue are read back into the days of Jesus. The gospels, it is maintained, tell us what the community taught rather than what Jesus said. The difficulty with this type of explanation is that it fails to account for the quite extraordinary freshness of the individual sayings and the genuine newness of the teaching of Jesus. Communities hand on and indeed elaborate traditional materials, but they do not create new and bold reinterpretations of the theology of the Old Testament, for that is nothing less than what the New Testament does. Somewhere there must have been an original mind behind such a penetrating new approach. What the name of that original genius could have been if it were not that of Jesus of Nazareth is a total mystery. The theory of community-manufacture as a sufficient explanation of the origin of the teaching attributed to Jesus has had a run of half a century or so and would appear to be almost life-expired, though the 'scribes' of the school will doubtless continue to quote the *dicta* of their Hillels and Shammais with all the reverence of the scribes who handed on the tradition of the elders. Jesus' injunction to call no man 'master' upon earth (Matt. 23.10) is relevant in every age of theological interpretation. To avoid misunderstanding it should perhaps be clearly stated at this point that no rejection of the methods of modern scientific biblical scholarship is implied here – textual criticism, literary criticism, form criticism and redaction criticism; it is necessary only to repudiate starting-points and assumptions which are not inherent in the scientific method itself.[8]

Although our four gospels were written in Greek and in a Gentile environment, they all give prominence to the conflict between Jesus and the Pharisees. It might have been supposed that outside Palestine the matters at issue in the conflict would have had little interest for people living in the Graeco-Roman world. But the evidence not only of the gospels but also of Acts and the Epistles of Paul shows conclusively that this was not so. The earliest Christian missionaries, many of them 'Hellenists' (Greek-speaking Jews of the Dispersion), naturally went first to the Jewish synagogues which were established in most of the cities of the eastern half of the Roman Empire. There they made converts, especially among the 'Godfearers', that is, Gentiles who, though unwilling to be circumcised, attended the synagogues, attracted by Jewish monotheism and high moral standards. Naturally there was a reaction against the Christian preachers amongst the orthodox Jews, who were, of course, of the Pharisee persuasion; they numbered amongst themselves keen proselytizers (cf. Matt. 23.15). Their 'proselytes of righteousness' were Gentiles converted to Judaism; they received circumcision, observed the whole Law of Moses and were deemed perfect Israelites. A Gentile who was thus circumcised changed not only his religion but also his race; he went on pilgrimage to the great feasts in the Temple (cf. Acts 2.10). It is hardly surprising that Paul should have been dogged by Jewish objectors in many of the cities in which he preached or that he should have had to defend his gospel in rabbinic-type disputations until he eventually did so in Rome (Acts 28.17-28). His letter to the Romans, written to a church he had not founded and not yet visited, is preoccupied with the Jewish-Christian issue. In these circumstances the Apostle of the Gentiles found himself in continual argument with his fellow-Jews, a struggle for which he was well equipped by his former life and training as a Pharisee (Acts 23.6; 26.5; Phil. 3.5). If he does not quote the sayings of Jesus against the Pharisees, that could be because he knew that his Jewish opponents did not recognize the authority of the Rabbi Jesus. Jesus' repudiation of the Pharisaic interpretation of the Law was what was in dispute, and Paul shows that he knows the mind of Jesus very well. Glorying in one's own ability to fulfil the demand of the all-holy God for righteousness is to reject the saving grace which is freely offered to the penitent sinner (Rom. 1-3): Paul is spelling out the deep meaning of the parable of the Pharisee and the Publican (Luke 18.19-13) in the only language which the sophisticated disciples of the Pharisees could understand.

Paul had constantly to strive to frustrate the efforts of the Judaizers to convert the members of his churches to Pharisaic orthodoxy. He was well aware of and valued very highly the efforts of the nameless teachers of the earliest Christian communities; these were the men and probably women who from the remembered sayings of Jesus first formulated the oral tradition which was communicated to the churches. They were of high standing in the ministry of the earliest communities (cf. I Cor. 12.28; Rom. 12.7; Eph. 4.11; Acts 13.1). The word 'teacher' (*didaskalos*) is the Greek equivalent of 'rabbi' and is used as such in forms of address to Jesus in the gospels (e.g. Matt. 19.16; 22.16; Mark 4.38; Luke 10.25; cf. John 1.38 : 'Rabbi, which is to say, being interpreted, *didaskalos*'). The word 'teacher', usually translated in our English versions by 'master', thus signifies the Christian equivalent of the Jewish rabbi, who taught his pupils orally. In an age when even amongst highly intelligent people reading and writing were not common accomplishments, the Christian teachers inevitably adopted the same teaching-method as that of the Pharisees, the only effective method in a non-literary society. They collected the sayings of the 'Master' on subjects which were of vital interest to the Christian communities, and, of course, because of the activities of the Judaizers, Jesus' sayings against the Pharisees were given special prominence. Doubtless the Christian teachers selected and arranged them for their special purpose, but if we remember the rabbinical insistence upon fidelity to the words of the master, there is little reason to question their general historical reliability. Mark, writing his gospel probably in Rome, perhaps as early as the days of the Neronian persecution (AD 64), gathers up the teaching tradition in the account of the dispute of Jesus with the Pharisees (7.1-23), and the theme of the conflict with the Pharisees appears constantly throughout his gospel from 2.1 to 12.40. Matthew, who is more likely to have been 'a scribe made a disciple of the kingdom of heaven' (Matt. 13.52) than the tax-collector of Matt. 9.9 and 10.3, compiled a gospel which is substantially a revised and enlarged edition of Mark's; he seems to have been a trained Pharisaic scribe, probably of the Dispersion, for he writes good Greek; he actually arranges the tradition of the teachers almost in the form of a New Law. It is instructive to note that the most severe attack upon the Pharisees in the gospels is to be found in his gospel (23.1-36). It is often said by those who approach the study of the New Testament documents from a literary rather than an historical point of view that Paul was not interested in the life and teaching of the Jesus of history. This is improbable in view of the fact that he ranks the teachers so highly on his lists of those whom he regards as God's gifts to his church for the work of ministering and for the building up of the body of Christ. It is gratuitous to suppose on the evidence of nine or ten letters, occasioned by theological or disciplinary questions which had arisen in the churches to which he wrote, that Paul was unaware of or uninterested in what was being taught concerning the encounters of Jesus with the sect of which as a zealous member he had formerly persecuted the Church (Phil. 3.5f.). One single verse is sufficient to disprove the theory that Paul did not know or care about what Jesus had said and done, and such a verse is to be found in I Cor. 9.14.

For the purpose of our enquiry it is important to understand that the chief opposition to the teaching of Jesus, both during his ministry in Palestine and subsequently in the Graeco-Roman world, came not from a political but from a religious source, even though it was a conspiracy of religious and political forces which contrived the condemnation and execution of Jesus. The Pharisees, whose name signifies 'the separated ones', prided themselves on maintaining their non-involvement in secular and political affairs, until at last, when they were provoked beyond endurance by the misrule of the later procurators, they gave their support to the Zealot revolt against the Romans in AD 66. The Sadducees, who had long depended upon the Romans, did not survive the destruction of Jerusalem in AD 70 and as a party they disappeared from history. Thenceforward Judaism was uniformly Pharisaic. Indeed the resilience of the Pharisees after the catastrophe was remarkable. The Temple had gone, with its priests and sacrifices, its crowds of pilgrims and its great feasts; henceforward for more than eighteen centuries the Jews had no national home. The Pharisees, however, kept alive the spirit of Judaism. They gathered at Jamnia, fourteen miles south of Jaffa (Joppa), where they continued their studies of the Law under Rabbi Johanan ben Zakkai. The national leadership was now in the hands of scholars. The 'Great Sanhedrin' which was established in Jamnia, consisting now only of Pharisees, was regarded by the Romans as officially representing the Jewish people. At Jamnia a Synod was held (c. AD 100) where according to some modern scholars the canon of the Hebrew scriptures was finally determined. But the rabbis found it difficult at times to concentrate on their scrolls and disputations because of the repressive policy of the occupying power, which was attempting to romanize Judea. The most renowned of the rabbis, Akiba (c. 50-132), the teacher of Rabbi Meir and thus an early progenitor of the Mishnah (the authoritative collection of the Jewish Oral Law), actively supported the guerilla operations begun by Simon Bar-Cochba in AD 132. The Emperor Hadrian (whose Wall is famous in Britain) had begun in AD 130 to build a new (Gentile) city upon the ruins of Jerusalem; he called it Aelia Capitolina (Aelius was his middle name), and he erected a temple of Jupiter, complete with statues of the god and of himself, on the site of the Temple. How deeply this act of profanation of the Holy City outraged the susceptibilities of the Jews and impaired their political judgment may be seen by the fact that Akiba, against all the inherited wisdom of the Pharisees, accepted Bar-Cochba as the Messiah and joined the revolt. He was captured by the Romans and burnt alive. Bar-Cochba's name means 'Son of a Star', perhaps the 'Star of David', for the Pharisees believed that the Messiah would be born of the rightful line of David (cf. Mark 12.35). His rebellion was the only significant messianic rising against the Romans. After severe fighting it was put down with great cruelty. Judea was virtually denuded of its Jewish population, and cities like Tiberias in Galilee, formerly despised by the Judeans as 'Galilee of the Gentiles' (I Macc. 5.15; Matt. 4.15), became their principal centres in Palestine. The revolt of Bar-Cochba, which was ended in AD 135, resulted in the exact opposite of what he had intended. Judaism, already widely dispersed, ceased effectively to have a homeland in Palestine, and thereafter was able to make its great contribution to the civilization of Europe, America and indeed of the world, by maintaining its Pharisaic ethical monotheism and emphasis upon 'separateness', in spite of pressures and persecutions, in those cities of the Gentiles in which it could find a refuge.

'THE PEOPLE OF THE LAND'

The religion of Galilee and Judea in the days of Jesus was Pharisaic, but not all of the people were Pharisees. The rabbis of the synagogues were trained in the Pharisaic interpretation of the Law, which they taught to the boys who attended the sabbath schools over which they presided. The education which the boys received (there were no schools for girls) was limited to one day in the week, but since it consisted of one subject only, it was thorough as far as it went.

23

The rabbis received no salary for their labours but earned their living by practising the trade which they had learnt as a condition of their ordination. Thus, Saul the rabbi, as a Christian missionary in later life, was able to dispense with the offerings of his congregations by practising his trade as a tent-maker (Acts 18.3; 20.34; I Cor. 4.12; 9.15; II Cor. 12.13). Jesus, if he was in any sense a rabbi by training, could have plied his trade as a carpenter (Mark 6.3). Unlike the Greeks, the Jews never considered manual work degrading. The Jewish population in Judea and Galilee held their rabbis in great respect, but the majority of them were not regular attenders at the synagogues, even if perhaps once in a lifetime they had gone up to Jerusalem to a feast. The business of earning a living and bringing up a family was complicated enough without the innumerable washings of hands and pots, the avoidance of 'unclean' foods and doing odd jobs on the sabbath, and all the other things which, as Jesus declared, were heavy burdens too grievous to be borne (Matt. 23.4). The strict observance of the ordinances of the 'tradition of the elders' was bearable for dedicated professionals, but for ordinary working folk who had to rub shoulders in the bazaars and places of business with 'unclean' strangers in a cosmopolitan city, the avoidance of defilement was an intolerable restraint on trade. This meant that the Pharisees regarded the average man-in-the-street, although he was a Jew, as a source of defilement with whom contact, especially table-fellowship, was prohibited. The Pharisees separated themselves from all unclean persons, that is, non-Jews and the non-synagogue-going majority of Jews. One of their chief objections to Jesus was not only that he did not keep the ceremonial law (cf. Mark 7.1–5) but that he and his disciples sat down to meat with 'publicans and sinners' (Mark 2.15f., etc.). 'Publicans' (in the English of Shakespeare[9] and of the King James Version of the Bible), from the Latin *publicani*, were the hated lackeys of the Romans who had purchased from the latter the right to farm the taxes in a given area and who therefore extorted from its inhabitants as much as they could. As tools of a foreign oppressor they were outcasts from Jewish society and were the most notorious of the class of people who, though Jews, were despised by the Pharisees as unclean. The scrupulous observers of the Law and the oral tradition were the *chaberim*, the true Israelites; the rest were the *'am ha-'arez*, 'the people of the land', who were regarded as worse than the heathen (cf. John 7.49 : 'This crowd, who do not know the Law, are accursed'). One rabbi (Nathan ben Jechiel) later wrote: '*Parush* (Pharisee) is one who separates himself from all uncleanness and from unclean food and from the people of the land, who are not scrupulous in respect of food.' The *chaber* ('fellow Jew', 'close associate'), whether learned or unlearned, was one who observed the law of tithing, levitical purity, sabbath observance, and so on, in all its rigour. The great offence of Jesus in the eyes of the Pharisees was that he mingled with 'the people of the land', taught them, told his parables to them, healed them and even sat down to meat with them. He could not even recognize a sinner when he saw one; he allowed himself to be touched by one, which proved that he was not a true prophet (Luke 7.39). He claimed to be able to forgive sinners (Luke 7.47-50) and chided the Pharisees on their unforgiving attitude. Moreover, he demonstrated his power to forgive sin by healing the sinner (Mark 2.10-12): God alone could forgive sins, since (on the accepted view) the sickness of a sufferer was a divine punishment for his wickedness. He gave special offence by his healings on the sabbath day (Mark 3.1-6; Luke 14.1-6; John 9.14). He even told a parable about how religious men – a priest and a Levite going about their sacred tasks – could not go to the aid of a man who had been left half dead by the *lēstai* who infested the Jericho road, because they would be defiled if they touched an unclean body, and how the sufferer was taken care of by – of all people – a Samaritan (Luke 10.30-37). St Luke, who records the parable, also bears witness to the fact that within the early Christian community the ancient prejudice against the Samaritans had been overcome, by including in his gospel the story of how the Samaritan whose leprosy had been healed returned to give thanks, unlike the other nine, who presumably were Jews (17.16); and in Acts 8 he relates how the apostolic preachers, having fled from Jerusalem because of the persecution which followed the death of Stephen, preached the gospel in many Samaritan villages, in one of which the hostile inhabitants had once refused to receive Jesus on his journey to Jerusalem (Luke 9.51-56). St John's account of the conversation of Jesus with the Samaritan woman (John 4.1-30) records the astonishment of the woman that a Jew should ask a Samaritan for a drink of water and the surprise of his disciples that Jesus should speak with a woman. But it is impossible to be sure whether the episode is in any sense founded on fact: the Fourth Evangelist so often appears to compose speeches, quite unlike the style of Jesus' utterances in the synoptic gospels, in order to bring out the truth

25

of history as John sees it, looking back over a considerable number of years. When John wrote, the Temple in Jerusalem was no longer a place where men worshipped. The true worship of God was not now bound to a locality, whether Mount Zion or Mount Gerizim (4.20-25). The other evangelists report that Jesus had prophesied that Jerusalem would be destroyed; John, knowing that the prophecy had been fulfilled in a total and terrible way, sees in the worship of Christ, now spread far beyond Judea and Samaria, the realization of the prophetic hope of Israel 'in spirit and in truth'. The ancient schism between Jews and Samaritans had become obsolete as far as the Church was concerned.

It was indeed an ancient schism. When after the Babylonian captivity the Jews were rebuilding the walls of Jerusalem, the Samaritans offered their help, which was brusquely refused. Having intermarried with the colonists who had been settled in Samaria by the invaders, the Samaritans were no longer deemed to be true Jews. They tried to prevent the rebuilding of Jerusalem (Ezra 4.7-24; Neh. 4.7-13) and subsequently sided with the enemies of the Jews whenever the latter were hard pressed. Excluded from the worship of the Temple in Jerusalem, they practised a form of Jehovah-worship, diluted by foreign influences, on their sacred mountain Gerizim, and maintained that they were the true upholders of the Law of Moses. Hostility against the Jews was the normal attitude of the Samaritans, and Galileans who took a short cut across their territory were sometimes murdered. The worst accusation the Jews could bring against Jesus was: 'Thou art a Samaritan and hast a devil' (John 8.48). It may be that the simplest explanation of the command of Jesus to his disciples setting out on their mission ('Enter not into any city of the Samaritans', Matt. 10.5) is that he was afraid for their safety; but, as always, more ingenious explanations are attractive to some scholars. The mission of Philip and the other evangelists (Acts 8.5-25) was not by any means completely or permanently successful. In later centuries the Samaritans were severely persecuted by the Romans and indeed by the Christian Emperor Justinian; nevertheless in the twentieth century a small community of them still survived and practised its ancient religion at Mount Gerizim.[10] The significance of the Samaritans from our point of view is that the various references to them in the gospels have a bearing upon the question whether Jesus can be said to have been nationalist in his outlook. The Jews had no dealings with the Samaritans, as

26

John, or an early copyist of his gospel, explains (John 4.9 and RV margin); the Christian tradition attests that in this respect Jesus did not share the nationalist sentiments of his fellow countrymen. ↙

II

THE POLITICAL INVOLVEMENT OF JESUS

That Jesus was executed by order of the Procurator Pontius Pilate is as well attested as any event in the ancient world, better even than that Socrates died by drinking hemlock at the order of the Athenian democratic assembly. Jesus was condemned on a political charge; the Romans would not have been interested in any other. The fact that he was executed by crucifixion is significant, because crucifixion was the punishment reserved for slaves but also for rebels amongst subject races. Moreover, the *titulus* over the cross in all four gospels describes him as 'the King of the Jews' (Mark 15.26, etc.). The mockery of the Roman soldiers likewise attests the ground of his accusation: Jesus died as a messianic pretender. It was the one charge upon which the Pharisees and the Roman authorities (with their Sadducean puppets in the Sanhedrin) could all unite. According to the gospels Pilate had his doubts in the matter, since Jesus did not look dangerous to him and the evidence was flimsy, but he could not risk a charge against himself that he was not Caesar's friend: here again John (19.13) brings out the truth of history, even if he composed the trial speeches himself. The cynical Pilate must have relished the spectacle of the Jewish leaders, now turned loyal to Caesar, bringing to him an alleged nationalist rebel, clamouring for his execution and asking for the release of a convicted disturber of the peace in return. His satisfaction, however, may have been tempered by the reflection that the popularity of Barabbas indicated that the unanimity of the Jewish leaders in condemning Jesus could not be taken as a sign that the Jewish people were ready to adopt a more friendly attitude towards Roman rule. However, the evidence in our possession is capable of a variety of interpretations, so that in all such matters any conclusions are inevitably open to challenge. The one reasonably sure statement that can be made is that it was as a

Jewish rebel leader that Jesus was liquidated by an improbable coalition of forces united against him. We must therefore consider the question of Jewish nationalism and ask whether evidence exists to show whether Jesus was sympathetic towards it.

JEWISH NATIONALISM

That nationalist feeling was strong amongst the Jews of the period cannot be doubted.[1] It would be surprising if it were not so amongst a proud and ancient people who drew strength from their own history in times of oppression. The example of the heroic Maccabeans who had thrown off the Seleucid yoke was still alive in the memory. The nation was united in believing that God's people should not be ruled by a heathen power, because Jehovah himself had expressly forbidden government by a foreigner (Deut. 17.15). The majority, however, taught by the Pharisees, regarded the presence of the Romans as a divine judgment upon their failure to keep the law of righteousness. Their resignation to this situation was doubtless reinforced by the realization that resistance to the army of occupation was futile. They were indeed conscious that it was wrong to pay taxes to a foreign government, which would spend the tribute of God's people on such things as heathen temples where images of pagan gods and of the emperor would be worshipped. Indeed, the detestation of taxes paid to the pagan overlord explains why the quisling *publicani* figured at the head of the roll of 'sinners'. It was in fact the original imposition of direct Roman taxation which sparked off the first revolt against the Roman occupation. Herod the Great had imposed heavy taxes, but at least he was half a Jew and was ostensibly a worshipper of Jehovah. The taxes had been paid, grudgingly as all taxes are, and indeed there was something to show for them in the vigorous measures which Herod had taken to curtail the depredations of the *lēstai* who raided the country from their mountain strongholds.

However, in AD 6 the Romans had deposed Herod's ineffectual son Archelaus and had assumed direct control of the government of Judea and Samaria. As in every other Roman province they immediately imposed taxation. The high priest of the day persuaded the people to submit not only to the tax but also to the enrolment necessary for the purpose of compiling a register of those liable to be

29

taxed. The census was an additional offence in Jewish eyes, because Jehovah's displeasure over David's sin of 'numbering' the people (II Sam. 24) was understood to involve a divine prohibition of all forms of taking a census. Less obsequious to the Romans than the high priest, one Judas the Gaulonite of Gamala, also called Judas of Galilee, raised a rebellion which was quickly put down by the Governor of Syria, Quirinius, called by Luke 'Cyrenius' (and so rendered in KJV; RV, Quirinius: Luke 2.1). Luke has got his dates wrong here, since Jesus would have been about ten years old in AD 6; he has also confused a local census with a universal one such as never took place in the reign of Caesar Augustus. A census by a Roman legate could not have been taken while an allied king such as Herod was on his throne, that is, at the probable time of Jesus' birth.[2] But these are not matters which need detain us here; we must recognize that Luke did not have the kind of research facilities available to modern historians. Luke in Acts 5.37 makes Gamaliel say that Judas perished in the revolt and that his followers were scattered. But here again Luke has not got his facts quite right. He says that the revolt of Judas followed that of Theudas, whereas in fact Theudas' insurrection occurred some ten years after the date of Gamaliel's speech to the Sanhedrin.

Judas of Galilee is often said in the text-books to be the founder of the Zealot party; the statement is repeated from one book to another, but there is no foundation for it. What the historian Josephus actually tells us is that Judas was the founder of something which he calls the 'fourth philosophy' (that is, alongside the 'philosophies' of the Sadducees, the Pharisees and the Essenes).[3] This 'philosophy' was distinguished from that of the Pharisees only by its insistence that God alone should be recognized as King and that therefore Caesar must be resisted by action as well as in word; its general agreement with Pharisaic teaching is indicated by the fact that Judas' chief supporter was a Pharisee named Zadok, who tradition says belonged to the school of Shammai the Strict. Clearly, therefore, the revolt of Judas was not messianic in character, since he did not aim at making himself king. In point of fact, though the books often suggest that a number of messianic pretenders arose during the Roman period, the first of whom we have any knowledge as proclaiming himself to be the expected Messiah was Bar-Cochba in AD 132. The revolutionaries, whoever they were, in the time of Jesus were not messianic pretenders. If Jesus is to be placed in a category of messianic pretenders, he is in a category consisting of only one member, so far as our knowledge goes; and the attempt to explain him as belonging to a class of rebels well known to historians breaks down. That there were rebels against Roman rule need not be doubted; perhaps some (not 'all') were looking for a king to slay their foes;[4] but the evidence that in the days of Jesus there was a general expectation of a militant messianic deliverer is lacking: Judaism, as we have noted, was dominated by the Pharisees who were politically quietist. There would be many who, like Simeon in Luke 2.25, were righteous (i.e. diligent in observing the Law) and devout, looking for the consolation of Israel. But such men did not put their trust in revolutionary action: God would deliver Israel in his good time.

As for Judas of Galilee himself, who perished in his revolt, he seems to have fathered a family with a tradition of revolution. Two of his sons were crucified by the Procurator Tiberius Alexander (c. AD 46-48). Another son, Menahem, was prominent as a leader of the Sicarii, who were practitioners of political assassination in Jerusalem shortly before the outbreak of the war in 66; he was killed by the party of the high priest. Our information about these men and their activities is derived from Josephus, whose two works referred to above are responsible for the extraordinary fact that more is known about the situation in Judea at this period than about any other province of the Roman Empire. But Josephus is not an impartial witness; he writes in order to persuade his Roman patrons that his fellow-Jews were really quite reasonable and well-disposed people who had been led astray by a minority of dissidents, and also to justify his own conduct in changing sides in the war of 66-70. The modern historian, part of whose professional expertise is the cross-examination of witnesses, must make his own assessment of the evidence of Josephus (or, for that matter, of the evangelists), while at the same time he must remain conscious of the fallibility of his own judgments in matters of great complexity, where such evidence as exists is capable of different interpretations.

THE LĒSTAI

One of the more obvious problems is to identify the groups which are described by Josephus as lēstai The word is opprobrious, meaning 'robbers', 'plunderers', 'brigands', 'pirates'. It is used in Mark 11.17 (followed by Matt. 21.13 and Luke 19.46) at the incident known as 'the Cleansing of the Temple', when Jesus, quoting Jer. 7.11, declares that the traders have made it 'a den of *lēstai*' (literally a brigands' cave). It is used by Luke, as we have already noted, in the parable of the Good Samaritan who took care of the traveller fallen among *lēstai* (10.20,36). John (alone) tells us that Barabbas was a *lēstēs* (18.40). Matthew (27.38,44) follows Mark (15.27) in reporting that Jesus was crucified between two *lēstai*, who reviled him: if they were nationalist guerillas, they presumably did not recognize Jesus as one of themselves. Luke (23.32f.) calls them 'evildoers' and does not use the word *lēstai*; he has his own story of the penitent thief, as Christian tradition has called one of them (23.39-43). Can it be, as some have suggested, that Luke, writing with a Roman–Gentile readership in mind, was careful to dissociate Jesus from the *lēstai* (understood in the sense of criminal nationalist rebels), thus under-lining the thrice-repeated assertion of Pilate that he found no evil in Jesus (23.13-22)? Mark, who does not avoid the word, was prob-ably also writing in Rome, but he was writing for the lower and lower-middle classes who spoke vulgar Greek and were cosmopolitan in their origins; whereas (even if Theophilus is a literary device rather than an individual: Luke 1.3, Acts 1.1) Luke was writing for the Roman upper class: 'Theophilus' is of equestrian rank. Has Luke's non-use of *lēstai* at the crucifixion any significance at all in the dis-cussion of Jesus' relationship to any guerilla rebel movements? We do not know, but it would seem somewhat precarious to find evidence here that Jesus was a nationalist sympathizer (not to say an active supporter of any guerilla movement).

More to the point, but equally inconclusive, is the question about who Barabbas was. The synoptic gospels speak of Barabbas as 'a notable prisoner', popular with the Jews (Matt. 27.16-26). Mark says that he had committed insurrection with murder (15.7), clearly con-trasting him with Jesus against whom no such crime could be alleged; Luke twice repeats Mark's statement about insurrection (adding, 'in the city') and murder (23.18,25). John alone describes Barabbas as a *lēstēs*, and 'robber' seems to be his meaning in view of the two other uses of the word in his gospel (10.1,8). The general emphasis of the gospels is upon the contrast between Jesus and Barabbas: whatever Barabbas was, rebel leader or common criminal, Jesus was not. The truth is that we know little about Barabbas; it is even possible for some critics to deny that there is any historical value in the story on the grounds that it is unlikely that Pilate would have released a dangerous criminal of any sort, and also that we know nothing from any other source about the alleged 'custom' of releasing a prisoner at the feast as a favour to the Jews. Perhaps the most significant use of the word *lēstēs* is one which is found in identical form in all three synoptics, when at his arrest in Gethsemane Jesus asks: 'Are you come out, as against a *lēstēs*, with swords and staves to seize me?' (Mark 14.48; Matt. 26.55; Luke 22.52). Is this a genuine word of the Lord, preserved by the disciples who were present, by which Jesus was repudiating the implied charge that he was a common marauder or alternatively a guerilla leader? In view of the fact that the word *lēstēs* is never used in the gospels in the latter sense, but always in the sense of robber or brigand, which is its normal meaning, it is unlikely that Jesus was protesting against his arrest as the leader of a militant nationalist faction. Indeed, if the gospel records have any historical value at all, it was precisely this evidence that his accusers lacked when they brought Jesus before Pilate and were driven to fall back upon the accusation that he claimed to be a rival king to Caesar. We have now mentioned all the instances of the occurrence of *lēstēs* in the gospels; it appears only once in the rest of the New Testament, namely, where Paul says that he was often in perils of *lēstai* during his missionary travels (II Cor. 11.26).

THE RELIABILITY OF THE GOSPEL PASSION STORIES

In the last resort the issue turns upon our general view of the historical reliability of the gospel records. If our study of them has led us to conclude that they are late compositions produced in an Hellenistic environment and designed to illustrate a Christology of which Jesus and his original Jewish followers knew nothing, we shall expect to learn from them a great deal about what the churches believed in later decades of the first century, but we shall hardly hope to find in them reliable information about the historical Jesus. However, this kind of hypothesis is most vulnerable when the Passion story is under consideration. There are two reasons for this. First, the earliest preachers of the resurrection of Jesus would have to meet the obvious objection to their claim that the crucified Jesus

33

Passion as historical + why

was indeed God's Messiah: he had been put to death as a criminal after trial by the Roman procurator himself, and there was clearly a case to be answered. It would therefore be essential for the earliest preachers to make a convincing reply to this objection. Their defence consisted in telling the story of how Jesus died; they let the facts speak for themselves. From the earliest years of the Christian mission the preaching of the gospel was a preaching of the cross and the resurrection. Along with the proclamation of the resurrection of Jesus the narration of the circumstances which led to his death, as we would expect, was an essential part of the Christian proclamation. This was the story which had (and still has) compelling power; the facts needed no argument and no adornment. Separated from the story of the Passion, the preaching of the resurrection would have been just as ineffective as were the claims of the mystery-religions which revolved around the myth of some unhistorical dying-and-rising god. The Christian faith differed from the mystery religions in proclaiming the resurrection of an actual historical figure, who had been seen and heard by multitudes of men and women who could still remember him. It all really happened 'under Pontius Pilate'.

The second reason for thinking that the accounts of the Passion in the gospels preserve a genuinely historical element is closely connected with the first. In all four gospels the Passion story constitutes the only part of them written in continuous narrative form. The other parts of the gospels (especially in the synoptics) are largely composed of short sections, more or less complete in themselves, arranged in order of subject-matter rather than in strict historical sequence, making any reconstruction of the actual course of Jesus' ministry highly conjectural. But with the entry of Jesus into Jerusalem on Palm Sunday all the gospel accounts come together and tell the same story with comparatively small variations. Even John, who for his own purposes has placed the episode of the cleansing of the Temple (2.13-22) at the beginning of Jesus' public ministry, tells recognizably the same story as the other gospels. He continues his practice of bringing out the significance of history by means of speeches put into the mouth of Jesus, as in the profound meditation on the political implications of the encounter of Jesus with Pilate, the local embodiment of political authority on the earth (18.33-19.16). But John shows that he knows the historical tradition concerning the trial of Jesus very well; he uses it to develop the theme of the relationship of the authority of Christ to the authority of the State as such. The unanimity of the accounts of the Passion in the gospels is strong evidence that the story had been formulated in the earliest tradition of the churches at an early date.

Of course, each of the evangelists tells the story in his own way and with his own purposes in mind. Mark, if he was writing in Rome, has a cosmopolitan audience in view and is not concerned to adapt his words to the susceptibilities of the ruling race, since as a member of a persecuted multi-racial body he could not hope to reach the aristocracy in Nero's capital. St Luke in his account of the Passion, as indeed throughout his second volume, Acts, makes a special effort to show that the Roman governors, including Pilate, had no fault to find with the behaviour of the Christians. His aim is to commend the Christian faith to the upper classes in Roman society. Matthew, writing for Jewish Christians, is much concerned to show that everything that was done had happened 'that the scriptures might be fulfilled'. Each of the evangelists is his own interpreter of the tradition (whether oral or written) which he had received, just as every historian in every age must give his own reinterpretation of the well-known historical sources. We would not expect the matter to be otherwise, and the historian's task today is likewise to make his own interpretation of the historical records. In the final resort it is true of all of us that 'every man is his own historian'. And in the matter of the trial and death of Jesus each of us has access to the primary historical documents, for there is nothing outside the New Testament which adds any substantial information to what the gospel writers have told us. Not even the articulately voluminous Josephus can help us here. His famous reference to Christ[5] ('a wise man, if indeed one should call him a man') is in the opinion of scholars the interpolation of a pious but misguided scribe in the second or third century. What Josephus actually wrote, if indeed he wrote anything on the subject, we shall probably never know.

THE CRUCIFIED MESSIAH

It is almost impossibly difficult for us to comprehend the offensiveness to Jewish ears of the preaching of a crucified Messiah (cf. I Cor. 1.23). Death by hanging brought upon a crucified man the curse of the Law (Deut. 21.23; cf. Gal. 3.13). A crucified carpenter-rabbi was

35

utterly at variance with the expectation, where it existed, of a glorious and triumphant prince of David's line, who would restore the kingdom to Israel, to say nothing of apocalyptic fantasies of a supernatural Heavenly Man who would slay his enemies with the breath of his mouth. The utter novelty of the Christian preaching is itself a strong argument in favour of the view that the idea must have originated with Jesus himself, though (as the New Testament implies) its full significance was not understood even by his disciples until after they had passed through the transforming experience of Eastertide. Of course, as the gospels make clear, Jesus had with unparalleled originality drastically reinterpreted the conception of the Messiah in the light of those Old Testament passages which contemporary Judaism did not regard as messianic prophecy, such as Isaiah 53 ('The Suffering Servant'). To say that this reinterpretation of the significance of Israel's history was the work of some unknown genius or of 'the community' is to abandon the attempt at serious historical explanation.

The distinguished Marburg scholar, Rudolf Bultmann, under the influence of the positivist conception of historiography dominant fifty years ago, at first denied that Jesus regarded himself as the Messiah,[6] and even in his major work on New Testament theology he disposed of 'the message of Jesus' in some thirty pages, which were then followed by some 570 pages on the theology of the early Church.[7] In this work, however, he conceded that Jesus appeared in the role of 'a messianic prophet', not merely as a teacher (rabbi),[8] though he would seem to prefer expressions drawn from existentialist philosophy, such as 'an eschatological phenomenon'.[9] Bultmann's widely influential theology, which substitutes existential awareness for the biblical idea of history as the *locus* of divine revelation, may be understandable in view of the widespread political disenchantment in Germany in the wake of the *Katastrophe* of 1945; and the ready adoption of his views by some American theologians may likewise express the disillusionment with American history amidst the bewilderment created by the war in Vietnam. Historians themselves demonstrate the inadequacy of the positivist conception of history as an objective science by showing themselves to be subject to the pressures of history in their own day.[10]

The question whether Jesus considered himself to be the Messiah is very important for our theme, because it is difficult to see what capital charge other than that of being a guerilla leader could have prevailed with the Roman procurator. Pilate's attitude towards a religious dispute would have been, 'Take him away and judge him according to your law', as John rightly sees (18.31). But the Sanhedrin had found no evidence, despite the suborned witnesses, that Jesus could be charged with rebellion against the State. However, the confession by Jesus himself that he was the expected Messiah (Mark 14.61f.; cf. 15.2 and parallels) could be made to serve, since 'Messiah' means 'the Anointed One' and therefore the divinely appointed King of Israel (cf. Mark 15.32). The secret, as yet dimly understood by the disciples themselves, was now out, though Jesus had made no public claims because of the danger of his being misunderstood and hailed as the leader of a nationalist movement. Does John in 6.15 in his characteristically allusive way hint that this was a serious danger to Jesus during his ministry, when, for instance, the would-be freedom-fighters wished to take him by force and make him 'king', i.e. the messianic deliverer from the tyranny of foreigners? Is this why the other evangelists represent Jesus as withdrawing from the multitudes amongst whom his 'mighty works' had created a strong sense of expectation (e.g. Mark 1.35-38)? We do not know the answers to such questions as these, but the gospels leave us with the impression that Jesus could easily have adopted the role of messianic leader if he had been so minded. But at this point we should remind ourselves that there is no evidence that any rebel leader before Bar-Cochba, over a hundred years later, had presented himself as a rebel Messiah. An occasional guerilla leader, like Theudas, may have 'given himself out to be somebody' – that is all that Gamaliel says (Acts 5.35) – but we are hardly entitled to describe him as a messianic leader. Even if there were those who imagined that Jesus would make a successful nationalist leader, it would not imply that they thought of him as the Messiah, any more than Jesus' refusal to lead an insurrection would imply that he was not aware of his messianic vocation.

The questions, mostly unanswerable, are innumerable. What was it that Judas betrayed to the high priestly authorities? What was the information for which these worldly men were willing to pay thirty pieces of silver? Not, surely, where they could pick up Jesus when he was not protected by the crowds with whom he was popular; their intelligence services could presumably have trailed him with his disciples to Gethsemane and identified him when they got there without the need to disburse a substantial sum of money. Was it, then, that Judas gave them the vital information which they needed, namely, that he claimed to be the Messiah, the rightful King of the Jews? Was this the secret which Judas betrayed, thus enabling the High Priest to ask the damaging question 'Are you the King of the Jews?' (Mark 15.2) or 'Tell us whether you are the Christ (Greek for Messiah), the Son of God' (Matt. 26.63; cf. Luke 22.67)? Much has been written upon the question of what precisely it was that Judas betrayed, and there is no certainty here; but it would seem reasonable to suppose that this corroboration of their suspicions or of the hearsay which was being bandied about, coming from one of the inner group of Jesus' disciples, would have given the Sanhedrin precisely the evidence it needed to take the case to Pilate. Confronted by the direct question, Jesus would either have to admit the charge or else be discredited in the eyes of his own disciples. A vigorous denial of the claim to messiahship would have meant that there would have been no Christian preaching in the form in which the New Testament presents it, whether Jesus had been acquitted or not.

The Sanhedrin found no evidence on which to hang a political charge against Jesus. There was talk about his having declared that he would destroy the Temple and build a new one without the labours of men's hands (Mark 14.58; 15.29); but the witnesses disagreed among themselves, and in any case Pilate would not be impressed by an idle threat of this kind. However, though Jesus could not be successfully charged with being a rebel leader because of lack of evidence, his confession that he was the bearer of the hope of Israel could be made to serve, since 'Messiah' and 'King of Israel' were synonymous terms (e.g. Mark 15.32; John 1.41,49). That Jesus claimed to be the rightful King of the Jews would be an accusation which Pilate would have to take seriously, since it involved a capital offence; his superiors might become alarmed if the Jews represented Pilate as being less than zealous for Caesar's sole lordship. John with his usual penetrating eye for the real issue brings out the truth of the matter when he makes the Jews (the Jews!) protest to Pilate, 'Everyone who makes himself a king is an enemy of Caesar' (19.12). The words may never actually have been spoken, but they form a telling instance of the supreme art of John as an historian in bringing out the significance of that paradoxical episode in Jewish history when the leaders of the nation compromised the meaning of the whole historical existence of Israel by doing a deal with Caesar in their determination to rid themselves of the threat to their own authority and prestige (cf. John 11.47-53). The Jewish leaders did not like the wording of the placard on the cross, 'the King of the Jews', and they tried unsuccessfully to have it toned down, but it was the price they had to pay for their success at court (John 19.19-22). Jesus died ostensibly as a rebel against Rome but actually because of his attack upon the pretensions of the religious authorities of Judaism (cf. John 19.11). John shows in the dialogue which he puts into the mouths of Jesus and Pilate the real issue which was at stake: the authority of Jesus and the nature of his kingship, which was not of this world, as over against all earthly political authority, typified by the power of Rome (18.33-38; 19.6-11).

All historical writing is interpretation, and all the historian can hope to do is to show that one interpretation of the evidence is better than another. This contemporary understanding of the nature of historical reconstruction does not in the least imply historical relativism. It recognizes that different interpretations are possible, as indeed is very obvious in dealing with the story of the trial and death of Jesus. We come to our own personal decision about the issue at stake when we find ourselves compelled by a particular interpretation of the evidence to conclude that this must have been the way things were: it happened like that. The four gospels, despite their considerable differences of standpoint and of content, cumulatively present a general outline of the way things were: either we find it convincing or we do not. It is not a question of getting down to the bare facts, for the 'facts' themselves as detailed in the gospels are already interpretations of the tradition of the preachers; the four evangelists have given to us their own reconstructions of 'what happened'. Since we cannot get at the tradition upon which they worked, though a critical examination of the texts may help us to catch glimpses of it here and there, we must not for that reason abandon our attempt to understand what they have told us. Each of them brings out in his own way what for him is the significance of the tradition. Being ancient and not modern historians they have no inhibitions about writing up the story so as to bring out what for them is the inner meaning of the events which they record. They exaggerate incidents or even invent them in order to illuminate what for them is the real meaning of the events, and one of the points which they wish to emphasize is that the primary responsibility for the crucifixion of Jesus lies with his Jewish enemies rather than with Pilate. John does this by means of the dialogue with Pilate. Matthew, whose attitude towards his fellow-Jews is ambivalent, does it by making the Jewish multitude respond to Pilate's hand-washing by crying 'His blood be upon us and on our children' (27.35; cf. Acts 5.28). In the light of our modern critical approach to the scriptures we can see what he intended, but in an uncritical and unhistorically-minded age his words, regarded as recording the curse of Holy Writ, had a calamitous effect in sanctioning the cruel persecutions of the Jews which have stained the history of the Church down the Christian centuries. Only in our own day has the light of the critical historical study of the Bible penetrated the darkness of ignorance and superstition and moved the more backward church authorities to reconsider the allegation of 'deicide' which had for centuries been brought against the whole Jewish race. Apart from the use of Matthew's words to justify persecution and ostracism, there was also involved the obscuring of the profound insight that it was human sinfulness as such, not some peculiarly Jewish depravity, which crucified the Son of God : it was my sin and my fellow-Christians' sin which resulted in the inevitability of Calvary.

The gospel writers present us with a coherent and convincing historical account of the way things were at the trial and death of Jesus. In line with the general conventions of ancient historiography, each of them underlines what he considers to be the significance of the story by adding his own editorial comment, sometimes even in the form of details which were probably not part of the original tradition. But that they preserved the general shape of the very early tradition of the Christian preachers seems to be the most likely explanation of their broad agreement upon the main outline of the Passion story. They agree in their testimony that Jesus' claim to be the Messiah was the critical issue upon which he was condemned both in the Sanhedrin and in Pilate's judgment hall, though for very different reasons in the two places. The Sanhedrin was concerned about the religious implication of Jesus' claim, which called in question the whole basis of their authority; but they astutely realized that this claim could be turned into a political accusation to which Pilate would have to listen. Knowing that he was already vulnerable because of his general misgovernment of the province, Pilate could not risk a charge of leniency in dealing with one who claimed to be a rival king to Caesar.

It used to be said that John had been in error in saying that the reason why the Sanhedrin had to take the case to Pilate was that it did not possess the legal right to carry out the death sentence (18.30f.), since there is no evidence apart from his that this was in fact the case. But, as we have noted, John repeatedly shows that he is very well informed about Jewish affairs in the period before the Jewish War. Moreover, the other evangelists all testify that the Jewish authorities did in fact consider it necessary to go to Pilate's tribunal. The truth of the matter would seem to be that Herod Antipas in Galilee could have carried out the death sentence, as he did upon John the Baptist and wished to do upon Jesus (Luke 13.31). This is why Jesus was at pains to avoid him. But in Judea and Samaria, which were under the rule of the procurators, the native courts were not granted the *jus gladii*, which the Romans reserved to themselves.[11]

SIMON THE ZEALOT

The theory that Jesus was a member of the Zealot movement is as old as New Testament criticism itself. H. S. Reimarus (1694-1768), with whom Albert Schweitzer opens his famous survey *The Quest of the Historical Jesus*, had already proposed the idea; the title of Schweitzer's work in the original German is *Von Reimarus zu Wrede*.[12] Robert Eisler in *The Messiah Jesus and John the Baptist* brought the thesis of Reimarus (that Jesus was a revolutionary) into prominence for a time; and more recently Paul Winter in his book *On the Trial of Jesus* has restated the argument.[13] It is, however, true to say that the idea of Jesus as a political revolutionary has not found favour with the great majority of New Testament scholars from Reimarus' day until now.

The original Bultmann school with its sceptical attitude towards the possibility of our knowledge of the historical Jesus would not have considered the question capable of profitable discussion, and with its devaluation of mere history (*Historie*) in favour of its existentialist conception of the truly historical (*Geschichte*), would not have been interested in such discussion, since the truly historical is what happens now in the 'eschatological' present. Even after the initiation by Ernst Käsemann in 1954[14] of the dubiously entitled 'new quest of the historical Jesus', the problem of the involvement of Jesus in the political situation of his times did not become a matter of urgent interest. Günther Bornkamm's *Jesus von Nazareth* was widely welcomed as a sign that the study of Jesus in his historical setting was not, after all, an impossible enterprise. Even so, Bornkamm is content to repeat that the party of the Zealots was founded 'on the first occasion of the taxing of the country' and that Barabbas was a Zealot.[15] He is emphatic that Jesus himself, though he was executed 'as one of the many messianic pretenders to the crown', was no Zealot and did not encourage the nationalist expectations which had been aroused by his coming.[16]

As we have noted, neither Josephus nor any other source supplies evidence for the existence of an organized party of revolutionaries called Zealots in the time of Jesus. If there were any messianic pretenders, we do not know their names or anything else about them; Barabbas would presumably not have been released by Pilate if he had claimed to be king of the Jews, since Pilate would then have been open to the same accusation of disloyalty to Caesar which he feared might be brought against him if he released Jesus. The fact is that the assumption that Jesus had relationships with a Zealot party is founded upon the soubriquet of one of the twelve disciples of whom we know nothing except his name: 'Simon called the Zealot' (Luke 6.15). The nickname is added to distinguish him from Simon whom Jesus called Peter (6.14). Luke is correctly translating into Greek (*zēlōtēs*) the Hebraic word 'cananaean' which appears in the lists of the Twelve in Matthew and Mark (10.4 and 3.18 respectively). This word has nothing to do with Canaan, as the translators of the King James Version supposed when they rendered it 'the Canaanite'; it means 'zealous', 'eager', 'enthusiastic', 'jealous'. The New English Bible inaccurately paraphrases Matt. 10.4 and Mark 3.18 as 'Simon, a member of the Zealot party', but at Luke 6.15 is content with 'Simon who was called the Zealot'. The only use of 'zealot' in the gospels is at Luke 6.15, but Luke repeats 'Simon the Zealot' in his list of the disciples in Acts (1.13). Luke does not use the word again until he records Paul's meeting with the Christian brethren in Jerusalem who told him that many Jews had become believers and that they were all 'zealots for the Law' (Acts 21.20). This is presumably a reference to the strict Pharisees and can hardly refer to a Zealot revolutionary party. Later Paul in his attempt to address the incensed Jews from the stair of the Antonine Tower described himself as a Jew of Tarsus, a pupil of Gamaliel, brought up according to the strict ancestral Law, and a zealot for God (Acts 22.3).

Clearly the word 'zealot' does not necessarily or even normally mean a member of the political revolutionary party of the Zealots. An examination of the related words (*zēlō*, 'to be jealous', 'eager'; *zēlos*, 'zeal', 'enthusiasm', 'jealousy') in the New Testament indicates the general sense of the word as having to do with religious zeal or religious sectarian rivalry (e.g. Acts 5.17; 7.9; 13.45; Rom. 10.2; I Cor. 3.3; Gal. 1.14; 4.17f.); the words are used in a favourable or unfavourable sense, according to what one is zealous for or jealous about, but they never refer to the Zealot party. Luke in Acts never refers to the Zealot party under that name.

It is a sobering thought that one of the Twelve Disciples, of whom no deed or word has been recorded, should have exercised such a powerful influence over modern scholarship. It is presumably upon Luke 6.15 that Käsemann bases his curious statement that 'Jesus converted Zealots'.[17] Since *zēlōtēs* is an ordinary Greek word, the translators of the English versions ought perhaps to have used an ordinary English equivalent, such as 'Simon called the Enthusiast'. In the New Testament the word refers throughout either to religious zeal or to religious rivalry and has no political overtones. We do not know what Luke intended, but probably the best guess is that Simon was a converted Pharisee of the stricter sort. There is some evidence that at an earlier period than the first century AD some *qannaim* (zealots) took action against lax Jews who did not observe the Law and forced them to do so, but they were not in any sense nationalist freedom fighters, since they attacked only Jews.[18] We also know that some Pharisees belonged to the strictest sect of enthusiasts for the Law; St Paul before his conversion was one of them (Acts 26.5), as he tells us himself (Phil. 3.5f.): like the *qannaim* of old he persecuted dissenting Jews, in this case the Christians, and he actually says that he advanced in the Jews' religion beyond many of his own age among his own countrymen, being more of a zealot (*zēlōtēs*) for his ancestral religion than they were (Gal. 1.14). It is incredible that he would have used the noun 'zealot' of himself, if it were widely understood to imply membership of a nationalist party of Zealots. It is still more incredible that Luke, writing (as is generally agreed) an apologia for the Roman ruling class, would have mentioned that Simon, one of the closest associates of Jesus, was a Zealot, if he had understood the term to mean a member of the party which had led the Jewish rebellion against Rome in AD 66. We must conclude that the New Testament, like Josephus, supplies no evidence for the existence of a political party called Zealots before the outbreak of the Jewish War.

Was Jesus a Revolutionary?

It would be an anachronism to read back into the time of Jesus the situation which later arose after the death of Herod Agrippa, when the misgovernment of successive procurators was driving the people towards the disastrous rebellion of AD 66. As Jesus grew to manhood, he must have heard many laments for Judas of Galilee, but there was no Judas Maccabeus in sight. It may be that some of the brigand chieftains, of whom Barabbas might have been a specimen, were astute enough to appeal to religious and nationalist sentiment amongst the people; but in favour of such a view there is only the negative evidence of Josephus, who exhausts his vocabulary of crime in cataloguing the wickedness of the *lēstai* in his attempt to assure his Roman readers that the Jews were not sympathetic to guerilla activities. In the days of Jesus only a fanatic would have dreamed of taking on the armed might of the legionaries, even if guerilla skirmishes might have occurred here and there. The people might be discontented, but they were realists, and their Pharisaic mentors counselled them to await God's good time. The 'fourth philosophy', if there were such a thing, was discredited by the fate of Judas of Galilee; heaven did not necessarily help those who helped themselves.

Nevertheless there was an air of expectancy abroad. Something was bound to happen. God would not desert his people. Their long history of tribulation and hope had conditioned them to look for the signs of a coming redemption. John the Baptist had proclaimed that God's reign was at hand and had invited men to prepare for it by undergoing his baptism of repentance for the remission of sins. Was John the promised Elijah who would first come to warn Israel that the judgment was about to begin (Matt. 17.9-13)? The expectation of the coming deliverance was vague and varied. Would the Davidic kingdom of old be restored in all its power and glory with the Lord's Anointed (the Davidic King-Messiah) restored to his thone, as the scribes of the Pharisees said (Mark 12.35)? Would he be a prophet, a new Moses, giving his people a new Law and leading them to the Promised Land (cf. Deut. 18.18; John 1.21,25;

Acts 3.22; 7.37)? Would he be a supernatural heavenly Son of Man, the fantastic figure of later Jewish apocalyptic imagination, a Messiah who would slay his enemies (Psalms of Solomon 17.21ff.) or a terrible 'Man from the Sea', annihilating the wicked with the flaming breath of his mouth (II Esdras 13 in the Apocrypha)? Perhaps the only kind of Messiah which cannot be found in the literature of the period would be the Che Guevara type, the guerilla hero of a Jewish resistance movement.

Jesus rejected every one of the current conceptions of messiahship. He had not come to restore the Davidic empire of a thousand years ago and he seems to reject the messianic designation of 'Son of David' (Mark 12.35-37), though the church subsequently saw in him the rightful heir of David's throne (cf. Rom. 1.3, etc.). He was reticent on the subject because even his own disciples could not dissociate the idea of the Messiah from that of political sovereignty (cf. Acts 1.6). In his parable of the Temptation in the Wilderness he told of his rejection of the Satanic suggestion that he should use his power to assume the political lordship over the kingdoms of the world (Matt. 3.8-10; Luke 4.5-8). And if at his examination before the High Priest he spoke in the poetic imagery of the day of his future coming on the clouds of heaven, he was affirming in language well understood in that age (and misunderstood by woodenly literalistic minds in ours) that his reign was not of the same category as those of the earthly political authorities (Mark 14.62): a reinterpreted conception of the messiahship indeed. He never spoke of slaying his enemies; he told his disciples to love theirs and to pray for those who persecuted them (Matt. 5.44). Though involved as deeply as any man in the political milieu of his times, his vocation was incompatible with the political attitudes of each of the Jewish sects of his day. He was no quietist like the Pharisees, content to leave things as they were until kingdom-come, provided that they were free to practise their elaborate religious code in aloofness from the political situation in which they lived. Still less was he willing, like the Sadducees, to live at ease in Zion, adapting the prophetic religion of Israel to the convenience of foreign overlords. Nor did he adopt a strategy of complete withdrawal from secular life, like the Essenes, who practised their austerities with complete disregard of their irrelevance to the lives of the common people.

When we consider the recorded sayings of Jesus which are some-

45

times quoted as evidence of his revolutionary intention, we find that alternative interpretations are more probable. 'Not peace but a sword' in both its contexts (Matt. 10.34-39; Luke 12.51-53) clearly refers to the division created in family life when a member accepted faith in Jesus; the saying would be preserved (especially in a Jewish milieu; the Gentiles were more tolerant) because it spoke to the actual situation of those who found themselves ostracized by their closest relatives and friends on account of their Christian allegiance (cf. Mark 10.29f.: the convert would acquire a new family in the church of Jesus Christ). The saying about the kingdom of heaven suffering violence and men of violence taking it by force (Matt. 11.12), recorded in a different form by Luke (16.16; from the time of John the Baptist 'the gospel of the kingdom of God is preached, and every man enters violently into it') is a famous crux for interpreters and many explanations have been offered. Some have suggested that the 'men of violence' are the Zealots, who seek to establish the kingdom of God by revolutionary action. But in that case are the words of Jesus intended as a rebuke?[19] In view of the lack of testimony to the existence of organized guerilla activity in the time of Jesus is this problematical saying sufficient to supply the lacking evidence? In its milder Lucan form it is possible that all that is meant is that the rejected common people ('sinners') are pressing eagerly into the kingdom (cf. Luke 15.1). But there is another possibility: the Greek text of Matt. 11.12 says nothing about 'men'. The *biastai* ('violent ones') who snatch at the kingdom of God may be the supernatural powers of evil with which the inbreaking reign of God had joined in deadly combat at the coming of Jesus: the 'strong man armed' is being despoiled by a stronger than he (Matt. 12.24-29; Luke 11.15-22).

If this is the only kind of evidence that can be found in the recorded sayings of Jesus to support the theory that he sympathized with any revolutionary movement which might have existed in his day, it can be countered by the great weight of his teaching about loving one's enemies, doing good to those who hate us, forgiving those who trespass against us, turning the other cheek, meekness, service of one's fellows, peace-makers, rejoicing under persecution, rejecting litigation, going the second mile (when the military compel a citizen to carry their equipment on the march), non-resistance to evil, giving one's cloak to the villain who has already taken one's coat, regarding even the Samaritans as one's neighbours or recognizing virtue in a Roman centurion. Jesus does not talk like a revolutionary leader, whether ancient or modern. As 'Che' Guevara is reported to have taught, revolutions cannot begin without first creating hatred of the 'oppressors'. The revolution which Jesus in fact accomplished was not a political one, though it has had important political consequences down the ages.

The only directly political utterance of Jesus is the pronouncement 'Render unto Caesar' at the conclusion of the story of the tribute money in Mark 12.13-17 (the parallel versions in Matt. 22.15-22 and Luke 20.22-26 may be regarded as the earliest commentaries upon it).[20] It was preserved in the Christian churches because it contained a word of the Lord upon the vexed question whether Christians should pay their taxes to the State (cf. Rom. 13.7; I Peter 2.13f.). There can be no doubt about its authenticity or its meaning. The Pharisees and Herodians had laid a cunning trap for Jesus. If he had said it was lawful (i.e. according to the Law of Moses) to pay tribute to Caesar, he would have offended the nationalist sentiments of the people and involved himself in argument with the scribes about the interpretation of the Law. If he had said it was not lawful, he could have been denounced to the Romans and convicted in a Gentile court. Sometimes it is said that Jesus cleverly extricated himself from the trap by a subtle evasion of the dilemma, but this is to miss the profundity of the answer which has so deeply influenced the development of the Church-State relationship in Christian history. Lord Acton said that Jesus' words 'gave to the civil power under the protection of conscience a sacredness it had never enjoyed and bounds it had never acknowledged: and they were the repudiation of absolutism and the inauguration of freedom'. There is genuine originality in Jesus' answer in the act of calling for a denarius (penny), for in current opinion coins were the personal property of the ruler whose image they bore: to pay the census (Latin: head-tax) was only giving Caesar what was his own. Coins of the type of the denarius which they brought to Jesus have been found all over the Middle East; this one would have borne the image of Caesar and the legend TIBERIUS CAESAR DIVI AUGUSTI FILIUS AUGUSTUS (or perhaps the superscription might have been written in Greek): both the image and the divine claim would have been unbearably offensive to the Jews. Unmoved by nationalist prejudice, Jesus asserts the duty of paying one's dues to the *de facto* authority responsible for law

47

and order, but without in any way reducing the claims of God. Judas of Galilee had raised an insurrection after the original imposition of the census: Jesus of Galilee was no upholder of the so-called 'fourth philosophy'.

The instruction to the disciples to provide themselves with swords on their future missionary journeys, along with other necessities for travellers on dangerous roads, is peculiar to Luke's Gospel (22.35-38). It seems awkwardly placed in its present context and perhaps is intended as a justification of what the missionaries had found to be necessary in the early years of their activity, despite the tradition about Jesus' injunction against carrying provisions on their missions during his lifetime (Luke 9.3; 10.4). It may have been placed here by Luke to account for the disciples' having swords at the arrest in Gethsemane (Luke 22.50). To suggest that Jesus was preparing for armed resistance to his arrest is unconvincing, since two swords would hardly have been adequate against well-armed troops. Eisler's assertion that the disciples meant that they had two swords *each* is absurd: eleven men encumbered by a sword in each hand would soon have been despatched by the soldiers. The incident of the arrest, when an unidentified bystander wounded the ear of a slave of the High Priest, is mentioned briefly by Mark (14.47), and the later evangelists elaborate the story as it was subsequently retold in the tradition. But the decisive argument against the suggestion that the disciples were prepared for armed resistance and actually put up a struggle is that the soldiers did not chase them but let them run away unhurt; they had taken Jesus prisoner and that was all that they were instructed to do. Their superiors were not interested in anyone else.

JESUS IN JERUSALEM

The tradition of the earliest Christian communities, as we learn from the critical study of the gospels, recounted the story of the last days of Jesus somewhat as follows. Eluding Herod Antipas in Galilee, Jesus set his face to go to Jerusalem (Luke 9.51); a prophet could not perish outside Jerusalem – that Jerusalem which he would have gathered as a hen gathers her chickens under her wing (Luke 13.33f.). When he drew near to the Holy City, he wept over it – and pronounced its doom (Luke 19.41-44). Jesus was a patriot, not a nationalist: God's kingdom would receive guests from the east and the west; they would have greater faith than he had found in Israel, whereas the 'sons of the kingdom' (the Jews) would be cast into outer darkness (Matt. 8.10-12; cf. Luke 7.9). Jesus told parables about the rejection of the chosen people and the incoming of the untouchables from the highways and hedges (Luke 14.23); the wicked husbandmen would be turned out and the vineyard would be given to others (Mark 12.9). Jerusalem was a barren fig tree, which produced a fine show of leaves but no fruits of righteousness (Mark 11.13f.). Like Jeremiah before him, Jesus was a patriot who was compelled to pronounce God's judgment upon the city which he loved: 'No man shall eat fruit of thee henceforward for ever' (ibid.). The Temple itself, in the possession of which the Jews boasted their security, would be cast down (Jer. 7.4-15; Luke 19.43f., etc.). It is not more surprising that Jesus should have prophesied the destruction of Jerusalem than that Jeremiah should have done so several centuries previously: mounting hostility to the foreign invaders and reliance upon false religious claims could lead only to military disaster. Hypocritical trust in their own righteousness prevented Jesus' contemporaries from discerning the clear signs of the times: they should agree with their (Roman) adversaries quickly while there was still time, before the inevitable penalty of resistance overtook them (Luke 12.54-59). But Jerusalem did not know the things which belonged to her peace. Of course, Luke was writing after AD 70, and thus he was able to touch up the adumbrations of Jesus with factual details about the siege of Jerusalem (19.42-44); but that is no reason to suppose that the prophetic eye of Jesus, unobscured by the mists of religious nationalism, should not, like Jeremiah before him, have discerned the inevitable outcome of the tension between sectarian fanaticism and imperialist lust for domination. The vultures – the Roman eagles – would gather round the carcase of Jerusalem (Luke 17.37).

With consummate skill Mark illustrates the truth that there were those who were ready to hail Jesus as Messiah, although Jesus himself had tried to avoid public curiosity about the subject because of the certainty of being misunderstood. Even his closest disciples could not assimilate his teaching about the vocation of the Messiah, which was not to triumph over his enemies but to suffer at their hands (cf. Mark 8.27-32). But the secret was out: at Jericho a blind man hailed Jesus as the Son of David, a messianic title (Mark

10.46-52). At the entry into Jerusalem, where amidst the excitement aroused by his coming effective teaching would have been impossible, Jesus gave a sign of the kind which had been adopted by the prophets of old. He rode into the Holy City on a humble ass, thus fulfilling the prophecy of Zech. 9.9, 'Rejoice greatly, O daughter of Zion ... Behold, your king comes to you: he is righteous and having salvation; meek and riding upon an ass, even upon a colt the foal of an ass'. (Mark's editor, mistaking the Hebrew parallelism, woodenly provides two asses, in order that the prophecy might be seen to be precisely fulfilled; he also supplies the quotation in full, which Mark does not: Matt. 21.1-11.) The meaning of the enacted parable was clear, since the Jews knew the scriptures of the prophets very well. Zion's king comes to claim his rightful inheritance; David's son comes to take possession of David's city; but he does not come to conquer it by force as David did. He is the meek and lowly one, not the conquering war-lord who rides upon a charger. His 'triumphal entry' is not like the 'triumph' of an emperor returning to his capital from a victorious campaign, leading the prisoners he had taken captive and bringing the spoils of war which he had taken. It is difficult to reconcile the manner of Jesus' entry into Jerusalem with any theory that he would have sympathized with the Zealot cause: Bar-Cochba, if his revolt had succeeded, would not have ridden into Jerusalem on an ass.

After spending the following night in the nearby village of Bethany (doubtless with a view to avoiding an assassin's dagger in the dark and overcrowded city), he returned on the next day to Jerusalem, where he visited the Temple. Here he gave another prophetic sign, traditionally known as the Cleansing of the Temple. Again, the significance of the sign would not be lost upon those who knew the prophetic writings. Jesus gave the sign of the prophet Malachi: 'The Lord whom you seek shall suddenly come to his Temple ... He shall sit as a refiner and purifier of silver ... (Mal. 3.1-6). He symbolically fulfils the prophecy, not indeed in any literalistic fashion, by turning out the currency dealers, whose extortions enriched the Sadducean hierarchy; and significantly he quotes Jeremiah (7.11). The incident, misinterpreted by those who search for evidence for their picture of Jesus the nationalist revolutionary, could have been nothing more than a gesture, an enacted parable: the money-changers would return as soon as Jesus and his followers had departed. No nationalist would have quoted (from Isa. 56.7) the words 'My house shall be called a house of prayer for all the nations (Gentiles)' (Mark 11.17) along with the words of Jeremiah. A violent demonstration by an armed band is out of the question here, because a cohort of Roman soldiers (at least 500 men) kept guard over the outer court of the Temple, where the incident took place, from the fortified Antonine Tower. They would have intervened, as they did when a tumult arose on the occasion of the visit of Paul (Acts 21.27-40); they would have come down the same stairs from which Paul made his defence. Josephus tells us that the Roman garrison was specially strengthened during the feasts. But Jesus was not arrested; in fact, we find him later in the week in argument with the chief priests, elders and scribes 'walking in the Temple' (Mark 11.27). The 'chief priests' and their associates would presumably have arrested Jesus if he had not had the protection of a considerable following of admirers, but they did not get their opportunity until the night on which Jesus did not withdraw to Bethany, deliberately remaining in the Holy City to break the bread with his disciples, as many other rabbis from Judea and the Dispersion were doing with their disciples at the same hour.

We need not delay over the statement in the Fourth Gospel that Jesus made a 'scourge of cords' with the object of driving out the sheep and oxen from the Temple precincts. There is no suggestion at all in John 2.15 that he used a whip for any other purpose than to clear out the animal sacrificial victims which were on sale. So hard put to it are those who wish to represent Jesus as willing to use violence that they speak of the whip as if it were a dagger and ignore the clear meaning of the text. In any case the Fourth Gospel is late in date and freely rewrites the tradition, even to the extent of placing the episode of the Temple-cleansing at the very beginning of Jesus' ministry and not at the end of it.

A careful examination of the early Christian tradition concerning the last week of the life of Jesus reveals a convincing and coherent narrative of the sequence of events which led to his death. There is no other evidence, and therefore the alternative to the acceptance of it is complete scepticism. What the evidence forbids is the reconstruction of the story with the object of showing that Jesus was a revolutionary nationalist who countenanced the use of violence against the Roman occupying forces. Still less credible is the view that he was himself a precursor of or a model for the guerilla leaders of our own times. We need point only to the utter contrast between

51

Jesus and the most widely adulated of the guerilla leaders of our age to see that the comparison is odious. Ernesto 'Che' Guevara, the professional guerilla of the Cuban revolution, of the Congo and elsewhere, was killed at the age of 39 when he was attempting to start a revolution in Bolivia in 1967. His hero-worshipping biographer Andrew Sinclair writes that he 'dedicated his life and death to the poorest of men without the help of God. The walls of the student halls of the world are chalked with the words, CHE LIVES.'[21] The students who started revolts all over the world in 1968 took him as their personal symbol. In the cult of Che he is regarded as a saviour, one who died for us: 'the photograph of his corpse is pinned as an eikon in many country homes across Catholic Latin America'. Che loved 'humanity' but he hated his enemies and killed other men for the sake of his cause. Che was a qualified doctor who forsook the healing profession. Jesus was a healer and never killed or injured anyone; he taught his disciples to love their enemies and to pray for their persecutors. Che left the world as he he found it; Jesus changed the whole course of history, giving to the world the noble heritage of the prophets of Israel, released from the bonds of the narrow legalism by which it had been obscured. No one died for Jesus during his earthly life (cf. John 17.12), but in a strikingly literal way Jesus died for Barabbas. He also died for Che Guevara. All over the world, nearly two thousand years after his birth, Christians gather to proclaim JESUS LIVES. Gamaliel's proposed test of the truth of the Easter preaching has now been running longer than any other socio-religious experiment that has ever been conducted (cf. Acts 5.38f.).

III

THE ATTITUDE OF THE EARLY CHURCH
TO POLITICAL AUTHORITY

The influence of Jesus on the course of history, including political history, did not end with his death upon the cross. Within a generation the message was proclaimed even beyond the bounds of the Roman Empire, JESUS LIVES. Ernest Renan, whose humanistic *Vie de Jésus* (1863) proved such a *succès de scandale*, after movingly describing the death of Jesus, breaks out into his famous apostrophe:

> Rest now in thy glory, noble pioneer! Thy work is done; thy divinity founded ... For thousands of years the world will extol thee. Banner of our contradictions, thou wilt be the sign around which will be fought the fiercest battles. A thousand times more living, a thousand times more loved since thy death than during the days of thy pilgrimage here below, thou wilt become to such a degree the corner-stone of humanity that to tear thy name from this world would be to shake it to its foundations. Between thee and God men will no longer distinguish. Complete conqueror of death, take possession of thy kingdom, whither, by the royal road thou hast traced, ages of adorers will follow thee.[1]

THE JERUSALEM CHURCH AND THE GENTILE MISSION

The theory that Jesus was a Zealot sympathizer has recently been brought into prominence by the studies of the late Professor S. G. F. Brandon of Manchester University.[2] In his earlier work, *The Fall of Jerusalem and the Christian Church*, he had maintained that there was a serious conflict between the teaching of the church in Jerusalem and the version of the Christian faith which was success-

53

fully propagated outside Judea by Paul and other leaders of the Gentile mission. In his *Jesus and the Zealots* he gathered up his argument and restated it, supporting it with an attempt to show that Jesus was a Zealot sympathizer: the leaders of the Jerusalem church were being faithful to the original teaching of Jesus when in the sixties they threw in their lot with the revolutionary faction and eventually perished with the Zealots in the catastrophe of AD 70. It should be noted that Dr Brandon's book was written by a scholar for scholars; it contains quotations and footnotes in seven languages, some of them untranslated. It is somewhat untidy and repetitive, being written with the single-minded enthusiasm of an academic for his thesis which makes the study of the scholarly mind so fascinating. Its author must have been disconcerted to find that he was quoted with approval by the leaders of the student revolutionary movements of 1968, who did not bring to the subject the academic detachment which the evaluation of evidence requires. Dr Brandon himself had served with distinction as a Chaplain to the Forces throughout World War II.

A brief summary of Brandon's wide-ranging and minutely detailed interpretation of the situation of the Jerusalem church before AD 70 can hardly do justice to his argument; yet his thesis cannot be ignored by those who seek to understand the political impact of the life and teaching of Jesus. He holds that the Jewish Christians in Jerusalem, where Jewish sects were not nonconformist, were distinguished from other Jews by their belief that Jesus of Nazareth, whom the Romans had crucified, would shortly return with supernatural power as the Messiah of Israel (198). (Numbers in brackets refer to pages in *Jesus and the Zealots*.) The duty of the Christians was to prepare their fellow-Jews for this supreme event. They had overcome their original hesitation about a *crucified* Messiah, having discovered in the scriptures the prophecies that the Messiah must suffer (19f., 179). Their attitude to the Romans was similar to that of the Zealots, with whom they shared sympathy for the poor and hatred for the rich and powerful, particularly the pro-Roman Sadducean aristocracy (199). The kingdom would be restored to Israel and the existing world order, as manifested in the Roman Emipre, would be ended by the coming of the Messiah; the judgment of the Gentiles would begin. 'Under the leadership of James, the brother of the Messiah Jesus, the movement included men accustomed to bear arms and ready to use them, and one at least was a Zealot' (205). (Simon 'the Zealot' recurs again and again throughout the book.)

The circumstances of the fate of James the brother of the Lord are obscure, since we cannot be certain of what Josephus said,[3] and the second-century Christian tradition is evidence only of what was being said a hundred years after the event. Two things are generally agreed: first, that James was so scrupulous in his fulfilment of the ritual Law that he was accorded by the Jews the title of 'the Righteous', and secondly that he was put to death in AD 62 at the instigation of the Sadducean High Priest Ananus by the decision of an unauthorized meeting of the Sanhedrin. Brandon does not consider the murder of James to be evidence of the unpopularity of the Christian minority but rather an indication that James was known to sympathize with the Zealot faction which detested the rich Sadducean aristocrats who supported the Romans and oppressed the poor (115-126; 359-364). According to Josephus the Procurator, Albinus (AD 62-64), rebuked Ananus and Herod Agrippa II deprived him of the high priesthood.

Brandon argues that the Jewish Christians joined with the Zealots, fought with them and shared their fate when the armies of Titus destroyed the Holy City in AD 70. He discounts the second-century tradition of the flight of the Christians to Pella,[4] a Hellenistic city in the Decapolis some sixty miles from Jerusalem; he considers it to be a legend, invented by Gentile Christians who in the second century had migrated to Aelia Capitolina (as the Holy City was then re-named), to justify their claim to represent the original church of Jerusalem (208-216). The Pella-flight legend had been a major factor in encouraging the belief that the Jerusalem Christians refused to be involved in Israel's struggle for freedom (210). He refers to his earlier argument that the flight of a whole community could not have taken place at any time between AD 66 and the start of the final siege of Jerusalem by Titus in AD 70.[5]

However that may be, a party of Zealots did manage to continue their resistance until AD 73 in the fortress of Masada on the Dead Sea coast. When the Romans finally broke into the fortress at Masada they found some 960 corpses of men, women and children (according to Josephus). The last survivors of the Zealots killed one another and their families rather than fall into the hands of the hated Romans. Even Josephus is moved to testify to the fanatical courage of the Zealots. The almost impregnable fortress of Masada

55

in its rocky fastness still bears its grim witness to the heroism, splendid and futile, of the Jewish nationalists and is today regarded in some quarters as a symbol of Israel's resurgence. But how many of the tourists who flock to the comfortable hotels, the cafés and saunas along the bathing beaches a few miles away, are mindful of the dark footnote concerning human courage and folly which history has inscribed upon its forbidding heights?

THE RELIGION OF JAMES AND THE GOSPEL OF PAUL

Professor Brandon's thesis involves the assumption that there was an irreconcilable opposition between the messianic nationalism of the Jerusalem church and the universalist gospel of the Pauline mission. For James, Peter and the original disciples, Jesus was the Messiah who would return in power and glory to restore the kingdom to Israel and mete out judgment upon the Gentile usurpers of the divine prerogatives. For Paul and the Gentile churches Jesus was not merely the Redeemer of Israel but the Saviour of the world: the scriptural promise was fulfilled in him, that out of Israel would come a light to lighten the Gentiles.

Brandon holds that, once the fact is established that the Jerusalem Christians fought alongside the Zealots, it follows that the original disciples of Jesus must have known that Jesus was a Zealot sympathizer and that they were carrying out his intention in their war against the Romans. Jesus never condemned the Zealots as he condemned the Pharisees (327); Brandon repeats throughout his book that the Zealot party was founded by Judas of Galilee and speaks of an active Zealot party in the days of Jesus (Simon the Zealot is quoted as evidence again and again). Did not Jesus adopt a Zealot slogan when he bade his disciples to take up their cross, since crucifixion was the punishment meted out to rebels (154, etc.)? Was he not himself crucified between two *lēstai*, whom Brandon assumes to be rebel guerillas (351)? Is it merely a coincidence that the attack upon the Temple hierarchy coincided with an uprising in Jerusalem (Barabbas, of course: Brandon assumes that the evangelists have covered up the involvement of Jesus in the affair)? 'The operation in the Temple apparently took place about the same time as an insurrection elsewhere in the city. This rising was undoubtedly instigated by the Zealots, and it is difficult to believe that it was quite unconnected with Jesus' action in the Temple, although the gospels mention no connection' (351). 'By attacking the system from which the sacerdotal aristocracy drew a considerable revenue, and by making some pronouncement of his intention to destroy the present ordering of the Temple and replace it by another more pure and holy, Jesus anticipated what the Zealots achieved in AD 66' (335), that is, when they gained control of the Temple and drew lots for a new high priest of their own liking. Jesus agreed with many of the views of the Zealots, 'but it would seem that his conviction about the imminence of God's kingdom, which would mean the end of Rome's sovereignty, caused him to be less concerned than the Zealots with the immediate prosecution of resistance to Rome. In the end, it would seem that the movement of Jesus and that of the Zealots converged in revolutionary action in Jerusalem' (356). For his part Jesus 'had no intention of surrendering himself voluntarily, as a kind of sacrificial victim, to his enemies' (351). 'The fact that he made sure that his disciples were armed is significant ... With how many swords the disciples were armed is immaterial; it is scarcely likely that it was only two, and the armament of the party sent to arrest Jesus suggests that Judas had given warning that the disciples were well armed and that armed resistance was to be expected' (340f.). If, as Brandon elsewhere suggests, 'Iscariot' is a corruption of *sicarius* (204n.), Judas was himself presumably a Zealot, in which case it is difficult to see why he should have betrayed Jesus: perhaps he was eager to precipitate a confrontation, being confident that Jesus must win.[6] Such conjectures are hardly the stuff out of which history is written. In our previous chapters the principal passages in the gospels to which Brandon alludes have already been considered, and it has been suggested that they form a reasonably consistent account of the events which culminated in the trial and condemnation of Jesus; it is not necessary to go over the ground again. Brandon's omissions are significant. For example, he remarks that 'the Gospels record no contact of Jesus with the Romans until he was brought before Pilate' (343). He nowhere refers to the episode of the Centurion's Servant (Matt. 8.5-13; Luke 7.1-10), in which the action and the words of Jesus are hardly those of a Zealot sympathizer. The story is from Q, a source which long antedates Mark's attempt (as Brandon supposes his gospel to be) to reassure the Romans after AD 70 that the Christian faith was not mixed up with revolutionary zealotism.

Although Brandon never says that Jesus himself was a card-carrying Zealot, he regards him as a martyr (albeit an involuntary one) for the nationalist cause against Rome. Jesus was not the founder of Christianity, as that word is generally understood, but of a sect of Christians in Jerusalem which affirmed that the brother of its leader James would return as the messianic deliverer to avenge the people of God upon their heathen oppressors and restore the kingdom to Israel. This sect perished in the catastrophe of AD 70, leaving behind it only a few remnants of despised Ebionite sects in Palestine and Syria, which held an attenuated (adoptionist) doctrine of the person of Christ, whose death had no saving significance: 'the Mother Church of Christianity is heard of no more, and the control and direction of the faith lay henceforth with the churches of the great cities of the Empire, with Rome, Antioch and Alexandria' (216f.). Thus, Professor Brandon reaches his sombre conclusion:

> And so the miserable remnants of the original form of Christianity, transformed by the catastrophe of AD 70 into despised and dying sects, continued to maintain the faith once expounded by Peter and James, the brother of the Lord. The 'gospel' of Paul, so signally rescued from oblivion by the Jewish overthrow, became the source of Catholic Christianity, in which the Messiah Jesus was metamorphosed into the Divine Saviour God of all mankind (217).

THE JEWISH OPPOSITION TO THE PAULINE GOSPEL

> The irony of the situation, from our point of view is that it is Paul's 'gospel' that has survived and is known to us from his own writings, whereas the 'gospel' of the Jerusalem Christians can only be reconstructed from what may be inferred from Paul's references to it and what may be culled, also by inference, from the Gospels and Acts.

So writes Brandon (154). No direct evidence concerning the doctrine of the Jerusalem church survived the destruction of the city. The question therefore is whether the evidence of the New Testament supports Brandon's hypothesis. There can be no doubt that throughout his ministry as the Apostle of the Gentiles Paul had to contend with Jewish objectors who could not grasp the truth that salvation resulted from the free grace of God rather than from the meritorious fulfilment of the works of the Law. In some churches, notably that in Rome, where the influence of Jews was strong (cf. Acts 28.17-28), he had to strive hard to prevent the Christian community from becoming merely a variant Jewish sect. It was to Rome that he addressed his major (perhaps his only) theological treatise even before he had visited the city, and it contains his deepest reflections on the relation of law and grace. Perhaps at Philippi there were Jewish Christians who controverted his teaching (Phil. 1.15; 3.18), and the 'foolish Galatians', troubled by the 'false brethren secretly brought in' as spies (Gal. 2.4), had to be reassured that Peter and James, 'the pillars', had given to himself and Barnabas the right hand of fellowship that they should go to the Gentiles (Gal. 2.9). At Corinth, where the church was being divided into sects, there was a 'Peter (Cephas) party' (I Cor. 1.12), but no hint is given about what it stood for. There is nothing at all in any of Paul's letters to suggest that Paul's opponents were emissaries of a pro-Zealot Jerusalem church and it is idle to suggest that the Jews of the Dispersion would have shared the antipathy of the Jerusalem nationalists for the Roman government under whose protection they lived (for the most part) peaceably, enjoying the privileges of Judaism as a *religio licita*, a permitted religion. There must have been others besides Saul of Tarsus who appreciated the status of Roman citizenship. Paul's correspondence indicates conclusively that his opponents were Pharisees. It is an anti-Pharisaic polemic that Paul is forced to conduct, and that is why he protests so vigorously that he himself has been brought up as a strict Pharisee (Phil. 3.5). After AD 66 the Pharisees in Jerusalem did indeed abandon their traditional attitude of non-involvement in the nationalist cause and fought with the Zealots on the outbreak of the rebellion; there is no reason to suppose that the Jews of the Dispersion, a decade or so earlier, would have abandoned the Pharisaic attitude that God would redeem Israel in his own good time. The Jewish opponents of the Gentile mission were Pharisees or half-converted Pharisaic Christians, and there is no support in the Pauline letters for Brandon's hypothesis. One well attested and indisputable piece of evidence in a field where hard evidence is scanty, although it is lightly dismissed in a single sentence by Brandon (171), is surely decisive on the question of the relations of the Gentile churches with the mother church of Jerusalem. It concerns the collection which Paul took up in his Gentile congregations for 'the poor saints' of Jerusalem (Gal. 2.10; Rom. 15.25-28,31; I Cor. 16.1-3; II Cor. 8.1-4; 9.1f.,12). In Acts 24.17 it is duly recorded that Paul brought the proceeds of the collection to Jerusalem on his final visit to the Holy City. Paul would hardly thus have exerted himself on behalf of a Zealot church which utterly rejected the whole basis of his life's work.

The evidence of the New Testament (and there is no other evidence) is that from its earliest days the Christian community was persecuted by the Jews, not by the Romans. Pilate would surely have hounded the minions of an executed rebel leader if he had considered them politically disaffected. In the early chapters of Acts it is the Jewish authorities who persecute the church, which consists of Peter and the other apostles with their followers. It was the Sanhedrin which arraigned Stephen (Acts 6.12,15). Saul the ardent Pharisee consented to his death and afterwards conducted on behalf of the authorities a search for Christians from house to house (Acts 8.1). Paul himself testifies to the persecution of the churches of God in Judea by the Jewish authorities, not by Zealot partisans (I Thess. 2.14-16), as one who had himself taken an active part in their harassment (I Cor. 15.9). The earliest persecution of the Christians by the Roman State is that of Nero after the fire of Rome (AD 64), when as an unpopular minority they became a convenient scapegoat. As Professor Hengel says,

> Until the Neronian persecution the Roman government took no more action against the Christians in Palestine [after the execution of Jesus]. The formation of the Christian community in Jerusalem shortly after the death of Jesus aroused only the attention of the Jewish, not the Roman authorities. The new messianic Jewish sect could spread, unmolested by the power of the Roman State. The crucifixion of the messianic pretender, Jesus, had closed the case as far as Pilate was concerned.[7]

The rapid spread of the Christian mission in the Roman Empire would not have been possible if it had been suspected of having any connection with a revolutionary faction in Judea. Even if we discount Luke's emphasis in Acts upon the favourable or at least neutral attitude of the Roman provincial governors towards Paul as an aspect of his apologia to the Roman aristocracy, it seems clear that the authorities had not received an official circular warning them to be on the watch for itinerant revolutionaries from Jerusalem. There is no evidence at all of the existence of a Zealot Christian movement in Jerusalem or anywhere else.

The assumption that Paul was the real founder of Christianity has been familiar since the rise of German Liberal Protestant theology in the nineteenth century. This was the era of the 'liberal' lives of Jesus, which tended to depict Jesus as a reformer who taught the two doctrines of the fatherhood of God and the brotherhood of man. The supernatural elements in the gospels were merely the first-century envelope in which the simple teaching of Jesus had been transmitted by those who had come to regard him as a divine Saviour, after the pattern of the oriental mystery religions domiciled in the Roman Empire. Paul was usually cast as the chief manipulator of the process by which the 'simple gospel' of Jesus had been trans-mogrified into the dying-and-rising god of the new mystery-cult which developed into second-century Catholicism. It was, however, generally conceded that Paul had understood a cardinal feature of the teaching of Jesus, namely, the doctrine of justification by faith, implicit in his repudiation of the Pharisaic doctrine of salvation by works of the Law; this was the element in Paul's teaching which stimulated Luther to recover the doctrine of salvation by faith alone, sadly obscured by medieval Catholicism. The recent school of Bultmann has brought this line of thought up to date by means of an existentialist interpretation of the gospel, which maintains a thoroughly sceptical attitude about the possibility of our knowledge of the historical Jesus while at the same time emphasizing the salvation ('authentic existence') attainable through the power of the cross: the cross confronts us with the necessity of existential decision. The cross as understood by the Bultmann school is not the cross of a Zealot martyr but that of the supreme representative of authentic human existence. Brandon's hypothesis devalues the cross and makes it merely one of the many pathetic memorials of brave men who have died for a forlorn nationalistic dream.

THE HISTORICAL ELEMENT IN THE GOSPELS

In the previous chapter it was suggested that the gospels give us a credible account, though incomplete in many details, of 'the way things were' in the events leading up to the trial and death of Jesus.

As against the historical scepticism of Bultmann it may be maintained that the devaluation of history as a source of revelation leads, despite his intention, to the ultimate in mystery-religions, an unknown figure that can be represented only by an X. Brandon takes a different line. The gospels do not support his interpretation of 'the way things were'; the evangelists must therefore have rewritten the story in the form of an apology addressed to Roman readers and designed to convince them that Jesus was not implicated in the Zealot movement which led to the War of AD 66-70. Accordingly he argues that in AD 71 or soon afterwards Mark wrote a version of the story to reassure empire loyalists that the Christians were not a rebellious political movement either in origin or in sympathy with the revolt (221-282). But Mark's apologia had consequences which extended far beyond its immediate concern. By explaining away the fundamental fact that Jesus had been executed by the Romans for sedition it made the crucifixion of Jesus a theological, not a political, problem (282).

The Romans in AD 71 had indeed given a splendid 'triumph' to the returning conquerors of Jerusalem, Vespasian (made Emperor in AD 70) and his son Titus, who finally entered the city and defiled the Temple, carrying off the sacred vessels. This act of sacrilege is what Brandon considers to lie behind the reference to 'the abomination of desolation standing where he ought not' (Mark 13.14; cf. Dan. 12.12f.). In the Roman triumph were carried the spoils of victory: the shewbread, the silver trumpets, and the seven-branched candlestick, still depicted on the Arch of Titus in Rome, under which to this day no devout Jew will go. They also struck coins commemorating the victory: the new Flavian dynasty (inaugurated by Vespasian) had need of favourable publicity by all the media of communication which were available in those days. Whether the Christians in their catacomb-existence after the Neronian persecution felt that this was the right time to call attention to themselves by issuing an apologia seems improbable. In any case Mark's Gospel, written in the vernacular Greek of one whose mother-tongue was Aramaic, reads more like a handbook for Christian teachers, bereft of their apostolic mentors after the persecution, than an apology addressed to persons of influence. In this it differs notably from Luke's Gospel, which (with Acts) is generally agreed to be addressed to the Roman upper classes; but Luke was probably writing at least a decade later at a time when he presumably judged the climate to be opportune. It must be concluded that Mark, if he intended an apologia, was doing his job unskilfully, because he retained in his story several damaging pieces of evidence, including 'Simon the Cananaean', if Brandon's interpretation of the soubriquet is correct. In Luke Pilate's elaborate hand-washing may indeed be an illustration of the evangelist's desire to stress the fact that the Procurator did not believe that Jesus was a serious threat to Caesar's sovereignty, but it hardly shows up the Roman governor in a good light; it is more likely to be a way of emphasizing the loyalty of the Christian Church to the Roman State than a disclaimer of the Zealot sympathies of Jesus, against whom his Jewish accusers had found it necessary to manufacture a political charge out of his self-testimony to his messiahship.

This last consideration is vital to the question of the historical reliability of the gospels and in particular to that of the credibility of the narratives of the trial of Jesus. If Jesus did not consider himself to be the expected Messiah, his 'good confession' (I Tim. 6.13) before the Sanhedrin and before Pontius Pilate is fictitious and the gospel accounts must be regarded as tendentious. In fact, we are left with the alternatives of Bultmann-type scepticism or Brandon-type invention. The theory that Jesus' messiahship was an artefact of the early Church arose in the hey-day of German Liberal Protestantism, when it was considered that the 'simple' (i.e. ethical) teaching of Jesus needed no supernatural or theological props to support it: 'we needs must love the highest when we see it'. Jesus, according to the Liberals, would not have accepted at their face value the naïve beliefs of his countrymen about messianic glory and the like. It was William Wrede, a professor at Breslau from 1895 until his death in 1906, who gave expression to the hypothesis that the historical Jesus did not regard himself as the Messiah; his messiahship was an invention of the post-resurrection church.[8] Mark's Gospel, according to this theory, seeks to explain the fact that the doctrine of the messiahship of Christ was not known to the earliest Christian preachers by means of the fiction that Jesus had enjoined secrecy about it upon his disciples. Wrede's theory was widely accepted by German New Testament scholars and became not so much an hypothesis to be tested as a category through which the whole teaching of the apostolic church must be seen. It destroys the credibility of the gospel tradition preserved in the synoptic records, and it is the basis of Bultmann-type historical scepticism and of the existentialist theology, which looks to the decision of faith rather than to history as the *locus* of revelation. It is, however, only a theory, and one which, like other theories, is time-conditioned. Its presuppositions are those of the Liberal Protestant school, which have never won universal acceptance, especially in Britain, and which are increasingly questioned by New Testament scholars today.[9]

If we do not begin from a presupposition which requires us to treat the gospels as tendentious, we find in them a tradition of the earliest 'eyewitnesses and ministers of the word' (Luke 1.2) from which, with the aid of critical-historical methods, we can discern a convincing outline of the course of events which culminated in the death of Jesus. Of course, we shall notice that each evangelist has his own way of telling the story and his own particular purposes in view in telling it. But we are unlikely to conclude that they were concerned to conceal the fact that Jesus was a Zealot at heart and to substitute a fictitious portrait of 'the pacific Christ'. The Jesus of the gospels is no creation of the Gentile Christian communities; it is founded upon Aramaic traditions, as Professor Jeremias' *New Testament Theology* makes clear. And if there are conflicting emphases in the gospel narratives, they will remind us that the tradition contained fragments from sources which reflect differing points of view. Thus, for instance, Matthew, an editor who is so far from being 'tendentious' that he is apt to gather up everything somewhat indiscriminately, reports a saying of Jesus which might indeed have come from the tradition of a very Jewish congregation: 'Give not that which is holy to the dogs, neither cast your pearls before the swine, lest haply they trample them under their feet, and turn and rend you' (Matt. 7.6). If the dogs are 'dogs of Gentiles' and the swine are 'unclean' beasts, we might at first sight think that we have here a Zealot-Christian saying about the Romans, who did indeed turn and rend the Jews in AD 70. But then we recall that 'dogs' and 'swine' as used of the Gentiles represented traditional Pharisaic, not specifically Zealot, attitudes. The saying would seem rather to have emanated from a Pharisaic half-Christian congregation, since it expresses Pharisaic political quietism in face of the certainty of Roman reprisals. And when we reflect that the saying, having no connection with its context, stands in Matthew's Sermon on the Mount, what are we to conclude but that he is an editor who somewhat uncritically gathers everything in – even here in the Sermon on the Mount! – without noticing that it breathes a different spirit from (say) the pro-Gentile stories of the centurion's servant or the Syrophoenican woman? One thing we cannot do with Matthew is to force him into a single mould. The tradition on which he draws is widely based, and we should be grateful for that. If the gospels are not 'straight' history, they contain the stuff upon which historians can go to work.

The evangelists are not historians in the modern sense. The very word 'evangelist' indicates that they were writing, as Luke remarks, in order to confirm the faith of those who had responded to the message of the preachers by tracing the course of the events in which that message had had its origin (Luke 1.1-4). In this sense they are not free from 'tendency'. But then, neither is Josephus. He is writing apologetic designed to convince the Romans that the Jews were not as a nation implacably hostile to the Roman State. Moreover, he had his own position to consider; he must have felt a certain embarrassment during the victory celebrations of AD 71 in Rome, when he saw the trophies from the Temple paraded through the streets. There was no going back to Judea for him; he had to find acceptance in Roman society. As an upper-class Pharisee he had joined in the rebellion when the Pharisees, against all their traditions, decided to support it. He became a commander in the Jewish army, but later (whether from prudence or from revulsion at the Zealot excesses) he defected to the Romans and was in fact appointed by them to negotiate terms of surrender with the rebels besieged in the Temple fortress. The terms were scornfully rejected and the inevitable massacre followed. Small wonder that he can find nothing bad enough to say against the Zealots,[10] whose fanaticism he represents as the sole cause of the final catastrophe. As a good Pharisee he blames the disaster on the Zealots and he regards it as divine judgment upon their having taken matters into their own hands and not trusted to God to deliver Jerusalem. Historians will know how to allow for his apologetic tendency, while at the same time they will acknowledge their rare good fortune in possessing an eyewitness account of the destruction of Jerusalem by one who played a prominent part in the struggle to the bitter end. From the point of view of our present interest he tells us nothing very significant. He knows about the murder of James in AD 62 at the instigation of Ananus the High Priest, but he does not seem to consider the Christian sect to have done anything specially worthy of mention. It may be that, after the renewed persecution of the church by the Jewish authorities, many of the leading Christians had fled from Jerusalem, as they had done on a former occasion when persecution had broken out (Acts 8.1,4). We do not know, because Josephus had no interest in the Christians, and conjecture is profitless. But we may be sure that, if they had fled, they would have found a welcome and been absorbed into those Christian congregations outside Judea which had established a reputation for hospitality to refugees.

THE UNIVERSAL GOSPEL

The New Testament bears witness to the fact that by the end of the first century AD, having taken root in many cities throughout the Roman Empire, the church constituted a new kind of society in which distinctions of race and class and wealth had been transcended on the basis of a common faith in Jesus Christ. All the books in the New Testament, written in widely separated places and by authors of quite distinctive approaches and backgrounds in widely differing circumstances, bear witness to the action of God in raising Christ from the dead as the fulfilment of his age-long purpose in Israel's history. That purpose, discerned by the prophets of Israel, was nothing less than the salvation of all mankind. Scholars have long been at work attempting to trace the development of this universal ('catholic') faith from the days of Jesus himself to those of the latest books in the canon of the New Testament, and they will doubtless be occupied with the investigation for many years to come, if only because the question is of vital importance for the understanding of the evolution of human ideas and civilization. Some hypotheses which have been suggested will be discarded, especially those which were inspired by the Zeitgeist of their own age and circumstances, however established they may have seemed to be in their day; historians, like other people, are not immune from the influences of the climate of opinion in their time. One hypothesis will doubtless always recur, namely, that Jesus himself is the ultimate originator of the new and bold reinterpretation of the Old Testament scheme of salvation, which is what the New Testament essentially is. Hellenistic influences there must have been, and in any case missionaries like Paul had to translate unfamiliar Hebraic terms and ideas into language which their Gentile hearers could understand. But that the basic concepts of the New Testament are derived from Jewish sources

66

and presented in the first place by Christian teachers of Jewish race would seem to be the direction in which the evidence of the New Testament points. Historically salvation is from the Jews (John 4.22), even though to the Jews as a nation the cross was a scandal (I Cor. 1.22). It was Jesus' own reinterpretation of messianic glory as manifested in suffering and service that set the Christian mission on its way after the disciples had experienced the power and illumination of his resurrection.

The steps by which the universal gospel came to be formulated cannot now be traced in detail. There is general agreement that the basic *kerygma* (proclamation) was in existence soon after the original disciples had been transformed by the Easter experience. It consisted in the affirmation that Jesus, who had been crucified, had been raised up by God; that he was therefore Lord and Christ, the Messiah foretold by the scriptures; that he would return in judgment, and that therefore everyone should repent and believe.[11] First preached by Jews of Palestine, it was received by many Jews of the Dispersion (as Luke's colourful and theologically motivated Pentecost story asserts). As a result of persecution in Jerusalem, the preachers went to Samaria and beyond; eventually some unnamed missionaries from Cyprus and Cyrene preached the Lord Jesus to Gentiles in Antioch in Syria (Acts 11.20). The Jerusalem church sent its representative Barnabas to report on the 'great number' of conversions in Antioch; he then went on to Tarsus to look for Saul (Paul), whom he brought back to Antioch, which later became the headquarters of Paul's Gentile mission. Thus, if Luke's narrative is at all correct, Paul was not the originator of the preaching to non-Jews. There is a great deal that Luke does not tell us which we would dearly like to know. Who first carried the gospel to Alexandria, where many thousands of Jews were settled? Alexandria was the second largest city in the Empire and Antioch was the third. For that matter Luke does not tell us who first brought the gospel to Rome. Was Alexandrian Christianity as defective as that of Apollos, who had come to Ephesus from that city, and did Apollos represent the teaching of Peter, as Brandon conjectures? (191-5). Brandon has to back up this conjecture with another, namely, that the 'other place' to which Peter went after his escape from prison was Alexandria (Acts 12.17; Brandon, 196f.). Luke leaves a great deal for scholars to conjecture, apart from their nagging suspicion that he has idealized the Church of apostolic days and covered up some of the divergences of thought and action which may have existed between the more conservative leaders of the Jerusalem congregation and the enthusiasts for mission, like those men of Cyprus and Cyrene whose unauthorized action in speaking to the Gentiles must be regarded as one of the decisive moments in the shaping of what was later to become European civilization.

Despite the opposition of Pharisaic Judaism both at home and abroad, the paradox remains that the gospel of Christ was given to the world by Jews of Palestine and mediated to the Gentiles chiefly by Jews of the Dispersion. A race which through centuries of struggle to preserve its identity had learned to express its apartness by means of an exclusive religion (in spite of the prophets) and by the meticulous observance of an elaborate moral and ritual code of law, had become the ground from which the new universal society had sprung. This new society was international, pacific and ready to minister to human need wherever it was found. Within a generation or two it had broken down the barriers of race, language and social status; and it was willing to co-operate with the Roman State in its divinely appointed responsibility of maintaining peace and justice amongst the peoples of its vast *imperium*. And all this was achieved in the name of the Jewish Christ who had suffered for all mankind and had 'left an example so that we should follow in his steps, who, when he was reviled, reviled not again, when he suffered threatened not, but committed his cause to him who judges righteously, who himself carried up our sins in his body to the tree [cross]....' (I Peter 2.21-24).[12]

THE NEW UNIVERSAL SOCIETY

The Christian Church was not merely a new society but a new kind of society. There is no real parallel to it in the history of religions. Its survival seemed improbable in the first three centuries of its existence, and its demise has been confidently predicted in many periods since then. Its congregations met in private houses for worship on Sundays, which were, of course, not yet holidays but working days, either before the day's labour had begun or after it ended. Sunday was chosen as 'the Lord's day' (Rev. 1.10) because every Sunday was an Easter Sunday, the weekly commemoration of the Lord's resurrection. The characteristic act of worship was the

68

breaking of bread (cf. Acts 20.9) in obedience to the Lord's command at his last supper with his disciples to 'do this' in remembrance of him (I Cor. 11.23-25): the Lord's resurrection had transformed the sad memorial of his death into an act of joyful eucharist (Greek for 'thanksgiving'). The 'business' of the local congregation would be dealt with, such as the relief of the aged, the sick and the poor (there were no social services in those days), and the worshippers would depart to their work or to their beds. To critics who have argued that it is only Paul who reports the Lord's command to 'do this', a sufficient reply is that all the churches of which we have any knowledge 'did this' and that this practice immediately became and has continued to be the characteristic act of Christian worship.

The earliest Christian churches thus had a highly distinctive form of worship; the so-called parallels of the sacred meals of the pagan mystery-religions bear no resemblance to this commemoration of a real historical figure who in no way fits into the mystery-pattern of a mythical dying-and-rising god. But there was no distinctively Christian ideology or ethical system or political programme. If the Christian 'way' had been tied to any such things, it would have become obsolete long ago, because ideologies, ethical systems and political programmes are epiphenomena of the social conditions and economic systems of their own age, and they pass away when times change. Such considerations do not mean that Christian insights have no relevance to or influence upon ideologies, ethical practices or political arrangements; it means that Christianity did not begin as an ideology, an ethic or a political programme, and that it has not drawn its continuing inspiration from such things. And if, all too often, Christian churches have conformed to the ideological presuppositions of their environment, this does not mean that Christianity itself is ideological in essence.

Christian religion did not come into the world as an ideology, nor can its continued existence be regarded (despite Karl Marx) as epiphenomenal upon social and economic conditions. It has persisted through many vicissitudes in the pattern of social, economic and political organization, adapting itself (for better or for worse) to its environment, yet in successive eras – ancient autocracy, medieval feudalism, modern capitalist or mixed economies – retaining its own recognizable identity or recovering it after it had been obscured. In the period of its expansion in the Roman Empire the Church took root in a social and economic order which was built upon slave labour, although we must not think of the institution of slavery in the ancient world in terms either of penal colonies (such as did exist, as, for instance, in the isle called Patmos; Rev. 1.9) or of deportees to the cotton plantations. The membership of the churches constituted a remarkable 'social mix'. Paul tells us that in his congregations there were not many who were learned, influential or of noble birth (I Cor. 1.26). The majority would be lower middle class, small tradesmen, artisans or shopkeepers, and there were also the slaves, the working class – the class whose only means of subsistence was not wages but a place in the household or on the estate of the master who owned them and their families. But there were also some learned members of the new society, which attracted people like Priscilla and Aquila in the days of Paul (Acts 18.2,26; Rom. 16.3; I Cor. 16.19) and philosophers like Justin Martyr in the second century. There were also some people of substance, in whose larger houses the congregation met to celebrate the Lord's Supper: the word 'church' did not refer to a building in New Testament times. There were also slave-owners as well as slaves, as we learn from the exhortations contained in the epistles, which are modelled upon the Stoic 'household codes' though they are obviously deeply Christianized: 'Slaves (*douloi*), be obedient to those who according to the flesh are your masters (*kurioi*, lords), with fear and trembling, in singleness of heart, as unto Christ; not in the way of eyeservice, as men-pleasers, but as slaves of Christ, doing the will of God from the heart, with good will doing service as to the Lord (*kurios*) and not to men, knowing that whatever good thing anyone does, he shall receive again from the Lord, whether he be slave or freeman. And you masters (*kurioi*), do the same things to them, forbearing threats, knowing that their Master (*kurios*) and yours is in heaven, and there is no respecting of persons with him' (Eph. 6.5-9; cf. Col. 3.22-25; I Peter 3.18-20). Slaves are not to take advantage of their masters because they are believers; such masters should be served the more diligently because they are believers and beloved (I Tim. 6.1f.). The new society could not change the whole basis of the workaday world of antiquity, but it could inject a new attitude of mutual respect and good will into the social system. In the little epistle which Paul sent to the believing Philemon concerning his runaway slave Onesimus we have a rare illustration of the Christian teaching in operation. And all this came about because of the example of Christ, who, though he was in the form of God, did not count equality with God as something to be snatched at, but emptied himself and took the form of a slave (*doulos*) ... and died according to the form of capital punishment which the State reserved for slaves as well as insurgents (cf. Phil. 2.5-8; I Peter 2.18-24). The Christian faith did not come into the ancient world as a new ideology expressing the social consciousness of either an upper or a lower class but as the restoration of true human relationships as such, the relationships which the class structure of ancient society (like societies in other ages) had impeded or destroyed. It did not preach the solidarity of the working class (slaves for the most part) or recommend militancy; instead it created a society in which right relationships amongst human beings, whatever their social position, could be restored. It supplied a motive and a power which could effect this restoration, the love of Christ.

Christianity did not bring into the ancient world a new ethical system. Although books bearing the title 'Christian Ethics' or some equivalent constantly appear, there is no such thing as a distinctively Christian moral system. Doubtless moral codes for the instruction of Christians are good and necessary in particular ages; the law of love needs to be spelt out in specific social contexts, always provided that Pharisaic-type legalism is avoided: salvation is not earned by fulfilling a code of morals. There is strictly no such thing as Christian ethics, because what is called the Christian ethic is really right human behaviour *qua* human and *qua* universal. Good action is good only if it is good for all men everywhere, the good which the sensitive human conscience universally recognizes, even while admitting that this is a standard beyond human reach. Here is truly the human predicament, recognized by Aristotle[13] as well as by the deepest prophetic insight of Israel (e.g. Ps. 51; Isa. 6.5; 58.2-8; 64.6, etc.) and by Paul (Rom. 7.18-24). Consciousness of moral failure is the first step towards accepting the divine salvation, and it is this consciousness which pharisaism (with a capital or a small p) is designed to suppress. Paul knew that conscience was a universal human phenomenon, as was also the guilty conscience; Jew and Gentile were alike guilty before the moral law (Rom. 3.23; 5.12). The Gentiles, though they did not possess the Law of Moses, still naturally did moral things and thus were their own lawgivers ('a law unto themselves'), their conscience accusing or excusing them accordingly, for the law was written on their hearts (Rom. 2.14f.). Or, as Jesus said, even the tax-gatherers and the Gentiles did the works of the law according to their lights; they followed the law of 'do as you would be done by' (Matt. 5.46-48). But he implied that 'according to one's lights' was not good enough: truly human behaviour would include such things as loving one's enemies as well as one's neighbour, turning the other cheek, going the second mile, and so on. These things were not to be done because they were specifically Christian but because they were human; they were the outworkings of human nature as God intended it to be. Jesus did not teach a distinctively 'Christian' ethic but asserted a standard of human behaviour *qua* human. He did not draw up a code of Christian ethics: the tree had to be good before it could produce the fruits of righteousness. Because Jesus is *the Man* (as the doctrine of his incarnation implies), his followers are to be fully human and should seek to attain the true dignity of humanity. The supernatural virtues, including faith, may indeed be attainable only through the gift of the spirit of Jesus, but they are none the less human virtues through which the fullness of the stature of Christ, that is, of human nature as such, must be manifested. The transmutation of the Stoic virtues by the standards of Christ gives us an excellent illustration of the relation of the virtues of the good pagan to those of the Christian congregations set amidst the social realities of the ancient world; the Christian leaders did not hesitate to adopt and adapt the Stoic 'household codes', because virtue is to be emulated wherever it is found, and Christians have no monopoly of it. They know that, judged by the standard of Jesus, when they have done all, they are unprofitable servants still: they have only done that which it was their duty to do (Luke 17.10).

Similarly the Christian churches developed no political programme of their own. This was not merely because they were in no position to do so but rather because the making of political programmes was in itself no part of their concern. They sketched no blueprints for Utopia. An influential strain in Christian thinking was indeed avowedly pessimistic about the prospects for this world; the apocalyptists held that things would get worse before they got better and that it was not until the cup of human wickedness was full to overflowing that the final judgment would begin with the return of Christ in glory. It is hardly surprising that some, like the seer John on Patmos, should read the signs of the times in the light of the gloomier prognostications of the Old Testament scriptures. In general, however, the Christian congregations settled down to the task of making the best of things as they were. They put no trust in political activism and formed no political programme, confident that God was in control of the affairs of the whole world and that in his wisdom he would consummate his age-long purpose of salvation for all mankind (cf. the expression 'the Saviour of the world' – the *kosmos* – not merely of the church: I John 4.14). They expressed this conviction by means of the symbol of the 'appearing' or the 'return' of Christ, an image appropriate to ancient cosmography and still capable of being understood in the age of astrophysics. Christians were even now citizens of a heavenly country, whose law was love and whose life was peace; but their present existence was like that of colonists far from their home country, whose duty and privilege it was to transplant the quality of the life of their homeland into the alien environment in which they found themselves. The political attitude of the Gentile churches can be found in a verse from one of Paul's last letters: 'Our citizenship is in heaven, from whence we wait for a Saviour, the Lord Jesus Christ' (Phil. 3.20). In the period of waiting the Christians, like good colonists, must be true representatives of their heavenly kingdom, establishing its patterns of behaviour in the land of their sojourning. In this world they were 'sojourners and pilgrims' (I Peter 2.11; cf. Heb. 11.13; Lev. 25.23). The 'Jerusalem above' was their motherland (Gal. 4.25f.).

The question is often asked why the church in the Roman world did not demand the abolition of slavery, surely one of the 'obscene structures of society' (to borrow a phrase of the revolutionary students of 1968). The answer, of course, is that classical civilization would be inconceivable without it; the whole social fabric would have collapsed. Aristotle held that the natural inferiority of the slave caste prevented slaves from rising above menial work, although in point of fact slaves often attained positions of high responsibility in their master's affairs, such as his commercial enterprises, the management of his estates and the ordering of his household. They even won great respect in the pursuits of civilization; the Stoic philosopher Epictetus was a slave. A grateful master occasionally gave a trusted slave his freedom, and freedmen are encountered in the counsels of empire. But of course, there were bad masters, and the lives of many slaves would be sheer drudgery; but even then the slave and his family were assured of a minimum level of subsistence. Slaves were often the descendants of captives taken in war, and these, because of their higher level of education and intelligence, were in considerable demand; they fetched high prices at the auctions and, being costly assets, they were treated with the care due to a valuable market commodity. Occasionally, however, we read of revolts of slaves who had been driven to violence by the conditions under which they lived; slave revolts were put down with the utmost cruelty. In a civilization thus constructed it is pointless to ask why the new, small and uninfluential congregations of the Christians did not abolish slavery. What they did, perhaps in the long run more important and certainly in the short run more constructive, was to recreate human relationships as between masters and slaves, who joined in the worship of the same Master in heaven, through the recognition that there could no more be slave (*doulos*) or free than there could be Jew or Gentile, or for that matter male or female, since all were one in Christ (Gal. 3.28). The new humanity in Christ was not to be achieved by any political strategy but as a by-product of faith in the Christ who himself had bidden his disciples to seek first God's kingdom and his righteousness, so that the blessings which the Gentiles vainly sought would be added as a free increment (Matt. 6.34; Luke 12.31 in their contexts).

THE EARTHLY AND THE HEAVENLY JERUSALEM

A consideration of the attitude of the Pauline churches towards Jerusalem is highly instructive. That Jerusalem should be held in veneration, not only as the historic focus of the people of Israel from which the Messiah had come but also as the place where the Lord had died and risen again, is not surprising. That they should have responded generously to Paul's appeal for alms on behalf of the struggling Jerusalem church, as Paul gratefully acknowledges, proves that they regarded themselves as indebted to the 'Mother Church' there. But the relationship was not a political one and the contribution of money was not tribute but a gift. As the Jerusalem church under persecution by the Jews was deprived of influence by the loss of its original leadership and eventually by the murder of James, the brother of the Lord, the significance of Jerusalem became more symbolic than tangible. Paul himself could hardly have retained any serious expectation of fruitful contact with the city after his unhappy experiences in Jerusalem on the occasion of his last visit to Jerusalem, which he left under armed escort on his way to

Caesar's tribunal. With the outbreak of the Jewish War the Jerusalem church faded from history, and a century or more afterwards the church of that city was composed of Gentiles. Nevertheless Jerusalem remained a symbol of God's dealings with his people and of the hope which they had given to the world. In the first century AD the Christian Church had no sacred scriptures of its own, and in the congregations the Hebrew scriptures were read every Sunday because of the promise which they contained that redemption should come from Zion. This promise had been fulfilled, and the Christian Church, now 'the Israel of God' (Gal. 6.16), could make its own the poignant expressions of love for Jerusalem which were found in the psalms sung in the congregations: 'If I forget thee, O Jerusalem, let my right hand forget her cunning' (Ps. 137.5; cf. Pss. 122, 125,126). Already the Christians sang the songs of Zion and even now participated in the worship of 'the Jerusalem which is above, the mother of us all' (Gal. 4.26). In the vision of John the Seer he saw 'the holy city, new Jerusalem, coming down out of heaven from God' (Rev. 21.2), a city in which the Gentiles walked and into which the kings of the earth brought their glory (21.24). Jerusalem was now no longer a political entity but a symbol of the blessedness of the redeemed. The city around which had been fought the sternest battles of Jewish nationalistic pride had now, against all probability, become the symbol of hope: through its open gates which never shut the glory and honour of the Gentiles was being brought (Rev. 21.26). In the strange imagery of the vision of John the Seer, the most intensely Jewish of all the writers in the New Testament, a river flows from the throne of God and the Lamb, and by the river stands a fruitful tree, 'and the leaves of the tree were for the healing of the Gentiles' (22.1f.). And down the Christian centuries Jerusalem has persisted as the symbol of the consummation of Israel's prophetic history, the promise made to Abraham, 'In thy seed shall all the nations of the earth be blessed' (Gen. 28.18; Gal. 3.8). Through St Bernard of Cluny to William Blake and today, Jerusalem, still in our times the storm-centre of fierce nationalistic rivalry, remains the ideal not of a political but of a universal human hope. During the lifetime of Paul, as he came to realize, the earthly Jerusalem had ceased to be a matter of political significance for the Church. The political reality with which he had to reckon was not Jerusalem but Rome.

Of course, in the Judaism of the Dispersion a parallel reorientation of sentiment towards the Holy City must have been taking place.

Pharisaic in outlook, the Jews, many of them comfortably at home and prosperous in the cities of their birth, could hardly have looked without consternation upon the growing tension between Jews and Romans in Judea. They were only too well aware how easily a pogrom or even an official persecution could be stirred up against their race. The Jerusalem which they cherished had always hitherto been for them the visible symbol of the historic destiny of Israel, and as such they venerated it and went on pilgrimage to it when they could. But the Jerusalem of the rebels was another matter. In AD 66 Menahem, the third son of Judas of Galilee (whose elder brothers had already been crucified in AD 48 by the Procurator Tiberius Alexander, himself a renegade Jew) seized the Temple, made a unilateral declaration of independence and assumed kingly (? messianic) authority; he was almost immediately murdered by rival priests. As Hengel says,

> Soon after the outbreak of the Jewish War the Zealot rebel party divided into several groups, which fought one another in a bloody civil war until Titus appeared before the gates of the city in the spring of AD 70. Here the words of Buchner from *Danton's Death* proved true: 'The revolution is like Saturn, it devours its own children.' The Zealots were in the position of driving Palestinian Judaism into a desperate war against Rome, but they were destroyed by the first concrete political problem posed for them: the question of the distribution and exercise of power.[14]

The Jews of the Dispersion must have shared the feelings of Josephus and like him decided that loyalty to Rome was the course of political wisdom; the Pharisaic tradition which they held in common with Josephus would have counselled them to leave the ultimate issue to the judgment of God. Thenceforward the Jews outside Palestine, like the Christians, sought to live at peace in the cities of the Empire; the only political reality with which they had to deal was the Roman State. Jerusalem became for them a symbol, as it did for the Christians, although many of them (unlike the Christians) expected that the prophecies of scripture would eventually be literally fulfilled in God's good time (e.g. Isa. 62). But it was a Christian Roman Emperor, Constantine, who about AD 325 inaugurated three centuries of the rebuilding of the heathen Aelia Capitolina, and it was Christian shrines which were then adorned. And still today the prophetic hope for the earthly Jerusalem seems as far from realization as it ever was: 'Violence shall no more be heard in thy land, desolation nor destruction within thy borders; thou shalt call thy walls Salvation, and thy gates Praise' (Isa. 60.18).

THE EMPEROR NERO AND THE PERSECUTION OF THE CHRISTIANS

There can be no doubt that the Gentile churches in New Testament times gave willing loyalty to the Roman State. They obeyed the government not merely for fear of punishment but also for conscience' sake (Rom. 13.5). Only at the point where obedience to the decree of a governor was deemed to be in conflict with their loyalty to God did they refuse to obey, and then they meekly suffered the penalty. Such a point was reached when the magistrate ordered them to give proof of their loyalty by worshipping the Emperor as divine: this was the accepted test of loyalty to the State. The suspicion of disloyalty arose because Christians did not attend public functions or the games on the state holidays, which were held in honour of the gods of Rome, including Caesar, 'son of God'. The oriental cult of ruler-worship, despised by Romans of the old republican tradition, had now invaded the West, and in the provinces it was especially cultivated by the local governors as a gratifying token of loyalty on the part of the subject populations. We do not know how many Christians suffered the full penalty for refusing to worship Caesar, but the allusions in the New Testament to their faithfulness under persecution suggest that the number was not inconsiderable during and after the reign of Nero (e.g. I Peter 4.14-16; II Tim. 2.12; Heb. 12.4-13; Rev. 2.10,13; etc.). Brandon's conjectural 'Zealot proverb' about taking up one's cross (Mark 8.34) should be set against the certainty that this saying of the Lord was preserved in the gospel tradition because of its relevance to the situation of the churches for which the evangelists wrote. Other sayings of Jesus were preserved because they were highly relevant to the actual life-situation of Christians under constant temptation to deny Christ before men (e.g. Matt. 5.10; 10.33). The penalty for a first offence of refusal to drop a pinch of incense on the flame before the Emperor's statue was to have the offending right hand chopped off, a barbarous penalty which would give a contemporary relevance to the saying of Jesus, 'If thy right hand offend thee, cut it off . . .' (Mark 9.43). Small wonder that the Christians avoided public buildings and law-courts, the circuses and the games in honour of the emperor, with the result that they became a little-known and therefore unpopular sect. Such a sect would naturally be an object of malicious gossip and would readily be suspected of performing obscene rites behind closed doors or even of plotting against the established order of society.

It was in such circumstances that the Emperor Nero found it convenient to select the Christians as a scapegoat when rumours began to circulate that he had himself started the great fire of Rome (AD 64) in order to make room for his own grandiose building plans. The Christians, who had hitherto sheltered under the privileges of Judaism as a *religio licita*, were now coming to be recognized as an independent sect which could therefore be persecuted without the protection of the law. In any case the mounting tension in Judea which led to the great Jewish revolt of AD 66 would do nothing to persuade the authorities to look upon them with favour, although it is unlikely that anything would have been known in Rome about a Christian Zealot faction in Jerusalem, even if one had existed. The Christians, unprotected by the law, had the misfortune to be conveniently at hand when Nero was looking round for a whipping-boy. Many of them were put to the torture; others were burnt; their leaders either perished in the persecution or fled from the city. It is probable (we cannot say more than that) that Paul was executed in a manner becoming to a Roman citizen, and even more probable that Peter was crucified (upside down, as the ancient tradition relates).[15] It is still a credible view that the earliest of our gospels was written by Mark in or near Rome for the use of the teachers of that church after their apostolic authorities had been taken from them.

Philosophers often discuss whether historians ought to pass moral judgments. With regard to Nero historians have in fact used a wide range of adjectives denoting moral depravity – vain, boastful, a lover of self-display (as charioteer or musician), extravagant, cruel, vengeful, timid, crafty, resentful, jealous, suspicious, licentious, voluptuous, dilettante: one in fact who believed in his own divine status and accepted the adulation of sycophants as his due. The court and the aristocracy suffered terribly under his tyranny. He had his mother, Agrippina, a sister of Caligula, cruelly murdered; his old tutor, the philosopher Seneca, was put to death, and the poet Lucan was another victim. It speaks well of the imperial administrative machine that it continued to function relatively efficiently in Nero's reign, which inevitably experienced its share of the vicis-situdes of Empire. The violent revolts of Boadicea in Britain in AD 61 and of the Jews in Judea five years later remind us of the immense burden of maintaining the *pax Romana* over such a vast and varied subject population. Though popular in the East, partly because of his patronage of all things Greek and also because of the success of his generals against the Parthian enemy, Nero was eventually declared a public enemy by the Roman Senate. He committed suicide at the age of thirty-one in AD 68, remarking 'What a genius perishes!' Such was the character of the Emperor who inaugurated the long age of intermittent persecution of the Christians by the State, which lasted until the conversion of Constantine. In the Eastern Empire a legend grew up that Nero was not dead but would return to take vengeance on his enemies. It is widely held that the *Nero redivivus* myth lies behind the cryptic allusion in the Apocalypse to the Beast which 'was, and is not, and shall come' (Rev. 17.8).

THE LOYALTY OF THE CHURCH TO THE ROMAN STATE

From the early days of its expansion into the Hellenistic world the Church maintained a loyal attitude towards the Roman supremacy. This attitude is all the more remarkable in view of the execution of Christ by order of a Roman governor on a charge of rebellion against Caesar. There could hardly be stronger proof that the early Chris-tians did not believe that Jesus was a political revolutionary, since they regarded his words and example as authoritative. The most lucid exposition of the Church's attitude towards the Roman State is found in Paul's letter to the Roman Christians (Rom. 13.1-7). The Epistle to the Romans was written before Paul had visited Rome, but not before Nero's accession (AD 54). In it Paul enjoins obedience to the government and respect for the rulers: 'Let every-one be in subjection to the higher powers (that is, the political authorities), for there is no power except from God' (Rom. 13.1). He instructs Christians to pay their lawful taxes (13.6f.). It is highly significant that these explicit and authoritative injunctions were given during the reign of the most corrupt emperor that Rome had ever known, one who regarded himself as a god. Paul's words do not imply extenuation of wickedness in an individual ruler or even

79

in a group of rulers. He is not speaking about particular rulers but about the institution of government, or of the State, as such. Probably he never contemplated the possibility of total corruption; the fact that he himself appealed to Caesar's tribunal indicates his confidence in the impartiality of Roman justice: 'I am now standing before Caesar's judgment seat, where I ought to be judged ... If none of the things of which they (the Jews) accuse me is true, no one can hand me over to them. I appeal to Caesar' (Acts 25.10f.). Perhaps the last word we hear from Paul himself is to be found in his letter to the Philippians, written during his confinement in Rome (cf. Phil. 1.13f.). He still hopes for release (2.24), but is serenely confident, whatever the outcome of his appeal (1.19-26). No whisper of complaint against the authorities who have confined him is found anywhere in his letter; there is no suggestion that they have not acted in conformity to the just laws of the State. His concluding message is, 'They that are of Caesar's household salute you' (4.22); it has reasonably been suggested that the 'saints' of Caesar's household are not eminent courtiers but his fellow-prisoners awaiting trial, just as it became current in English to refer to prisoners as 'His Majesty's guests'.[16] There is endless discussion but no certainty about what happened to Paul after that. It is unlikely that he escaped the fate of Nero's many victims and it is probable that he never reached Caesar's tribunal at all. The letters to Timothy and Titus probably contain genuine fragments of Paul's correspondence (who except Paul himself would have made him say 'sinners of whom I am chief'? I Tim. 1.15), but as they stand, they would seem to have been put together by someone who, confronted by a situation considerably later than that of Paul's day, was trying to reassert Paul's authority amidst the clamour of conflicting voices. Such devices seem strange to our modern ways of thinking, but in the ancient world it was an acceptable practice to write in the name of a revered teacher to convey what his ardent disciples judged would have been his mind in the new situation that had arisen.

Paul therefore cannot be quoted as representing the attitude of the Church towards the political authority of Rome after the persecution of Nero. There is, however, clear evidence in the New Testament that the Church's attitude remained unchanged. Whether the words of I Tim. 2.1-3 are from a genuine fragment of Paul's correspondence or whether they were written after his death by the compiler of the epistle as we now have it, they testify to the practice of offering prayer for the State:

> I exhort, therefore, first of all, that supplications, prayers, intercessions and thanksgivings (*eucharistias*) be made for all men: for kings and all that are in high place, that we may lead a tranquil and quiet life in all godliness and honesty. This is good and acceptable in the sight of God our Saviour.

The fact that I Timothy was accepted as Pauline and was included in the canon of New Testament scriptures is sufficient evidence that during the years of persecution prayers for the State were said in the meetings of the congregations. Matthew's gospel was undoubtedly written at some date considerably later than Nero's reign, and it includes sayings of Jesus which were highly relevant to the situation of a persecuted church: 'pray for those who persecute you' (5.44; cf. 5.11,39; 6.12,14f.). The Fourth Evangelist provides similar evidence: 'a slave (*doulos*) is not greater than his owner (*kurios*); if they persecuted me, they will also persecute you' (John 15.20, quoted as a remembered word of Jesus). The same writer (or a disciple of his) insists that the 'new commandment' of love shall rule in all the inner relationships of the ostracized congregations: 'Marvel not, brethren, if the world hates you: we know that we have passed out of death into life, because we love the brethren' (I John 3.13f.). The Jewish–Christian Epistle of James (whoever he was: he makes no claim to be the brother of the Lord) likewise stresses the duty of patient endurance under temptation and suffering and of the avoidance of social distinctions amongst the brethren until the coming (*parousia*) of the Lord (5.7-11). The First Epistle of Peter, about whose precise authorship and date we know tantalizingly little, speaks of the political duty of Christians in very strong terms: 'Be subject to every ordinance of man for the Lord's sake: whether it be to the king as supreme, or to governors as sent by him for vengeance on evildoers and for the praise of those who do right ... Honour all men. Love the brotherhood. Fear God. Honour the king' (2.13f.,17).

At I Peter 4.15 a new beginning seems to be made after the apparently concluding doxology of the previous verse; some scholars think that it is the opening verse of another letter which has been added on to the one which ended at 4.14. It speaks of a new situation in the church to which it is addressed, namely, the outbreak of active persecution, such as is not envisaged in the earlier part:

> Beloved, think it not strange concerning the fiery trial among you, which comes upon you to test you ... Inasmuch as you are partakers of Christ's sufferings, rejoice ... If you are reproached for the name of Christ, you are blessed ... Let none of you suffer as a murderer, thief or evildoer, or as a meddler in other men's affairs [? as a political agitator]; but if any man suffer as a Christian, let him not be ashamed, but let him glorify God in this name. For the time is come for judgment to begin in the house of God ... (4.12-17).

Here we have explicit evidence of the persecution of the churches by some magistrates on the sole ground of allegiance to Christ, such as did not take place before Nero's reign. We cannot be certain when or where such persecutions of Christians simply as Christians first began; we do not know to which church the 'general' epistle of Peter was addressed. What we do know is that this pattern of persecution, sometimes quiescent, sometimes severe, was repeated in various parts of the Empire for more than two centuries.[17]

THE DARKER FACE OF ROME

One of the latest of the New Testament writings presents an insight into the nature of political authority which is strikingly different from the positive view of the State as an aspect of the beneficent divine ordering of the world which we find in Rom. 13.1-7. But then, the circumstances of Paul, protected by his Roman citizenship in the years before Nero's persecution, were strikingly different from those of John the Seer, committed to penal slavery on the isle of Patmos in the days of the persecuting Emperor Domitian (51-96), who succeeded his brother Titus in AD 81. The Apocalypse of John (the word Apocalypse is Greek for Revelation) was not in the opinion of most scholars the work of the apostle John but of a Jewish Christian who belonged to the 'order' of Christian prophets (cf. I Cor. 12.28; Eph. 4.11) and who thought in images drawn from Jewish apocalyptic. A chief characteristic of the latter was its belief that the increasing calamities of the times would shortly culminate in the End of the Age and the coming Judgment and Reign of God. To us the imagery seems bizarre, but to the Christian Jews it would have the advantage of being unintelligible to the State police if it fell into their hands. A leading theme of the Johannine Apocalypse is the necessity of remaining faithful to Christ in a time of severe persecution. Nero's persecution had not affected Asia Minor, but that of Domitian had a longer reach. In the view of many scholars, Nero is the Beast from the Sea (Rev. 13.1ff.), who made war on the saints; Domitian is the second Beast (13.11) and is probably to be identified with the *Nero redivivus* 'whose death-stroke was healed' (13.12). He caused all those who would not worship the image of the Beast (i.e. the Emperor) to be killed (13.15). The 'number of the Beast', 666, is held by many scholars to be a cryptogram (in Hebrew numeration) of Nero Caesar (13.18). In the following chapter 'Babylon the great, who has made all the nations to drink of the wine of her fornication' (an Old Testament metaphor for idolatry, 'whoring after false gods'), is Rome, upon which the final judgment of God is pronounced. The whole earth is cast into the great wine-press of the wrath of God (14.19).

The Apocalypse of John was received into the canon of Christian scripture only gradually, especially in the East. This was doubtless because its Hebraic imagery was not understood and its millenarian speculations were not generally acceptable in the Gentile churches. Nevertheless we may regard it as providential that the Apocalypse was eventually included in the Church's Bible, for it contains an essential biblical insight into the character of political authority. From beginning to end the Old Testament is constantly aware of the darker face of Empire. From Nimrod, the 'mighty hunter', who built Nineveh and whose name became proverbial when conquerors were spoken of (Gen. 10.9), to the Assyrians whom Yahweh raised up to chastise Israel (Isa. 10.5-19), to the Prince of Tyre who set up his imperial power as if he were God (Ezek. 28.1-10), to Babylon itself, whose very name remained for centuries the symbol of brutal domination, or to Antiochus Epiphanes, the original 'abomination of desolation' (Dan. 9.28; 11.31), the Old Testament teaches that the power which derives from God has been used by heathen overlords for their own aggrandisement and not for the righteous purpose of orderly rule and enrichment of life for which it was instituted by God. This is the aspect of political authority which is appropriately described as *demonic*: that which is good and beneficent becomes inextricably entangled with that which is evil and cruel. John the Seer understands the Old Testament doctrine of the State very well.

Power is given to men, but they abuse it to pervert the benign purpose for which it was ordained. Rome is Babylon, and in his vision he foresees her fall. God's purpose will be fulfilled not by the political agency of Rome but through the coming down of the New Jerusalem from heaven to earth (Rev. 21).

John is indeed the most 'Jewish' writer in the New Testament, but he is utterly universalist in outlook. The great multitude, which he sees in his vision of those who stand before the throne and before the Lamb, are from every nation and from all tribes and peoples and languages (Rev. 7.9). In contrast to those who worship the Beast – the sycophantic crowds who sing praises in honour of the Emperor at the games – they sing a new song which (in the opinion of some scholars) is a parody of the very hymns which were addressed to Caesar: not Caesar, but God, is worshipped as the one who sits upon the throne and is worthy to receive 'blessing and glory and wisdom and thanksgiving (*eucharistia*) and power and might ... for ever and ever' (7.12). The hymns are sung by the martyrs who came out of great tribulation (the persecution) and washed their robes and made them white in the blood of the Lamb (7.14). The one who 'overcomes' (the *victor ludorum*) in the cosmic contest goes to the victor's seat, not in the Emperor's stall where he feasts upon the royal delicacies, but in the Father's throne (3.21) to eat the fruit of the tree of life in the paradise of God (2.7). The one who overcomes receives not the garland (*stephanos*) of the winner of the Games but the crown (*stephanos*) of life, because he has been faithful unto death (2.10). The flattering court poets composed odes to Domitian, who called himself *Dominus et Deus* and toured the cities of the Empire, providing lavish banquets and spectacular circuses and games at which he was accorded divine honours. The people prepared a conqueror's *adventus* ('triumph'), even when his generals had won no victories. He was hailed by Statius as the bringer of the eternal light, 'brighter than the morning star', the inaugurator of the new age. The poet Martial sang, 'Morning Star, bring on the Day: come soon, let us not fear: Rome prays that Caesar may soon appear.' But John hears the testimony of Jesus: 'I am the bright, the morning star' (22.16) and receives the promise that Jesus will soon appear. He closes his book of Christian prophecy with the prayer, 'Amen: come, Lord Jesus' (22.20).

The book of Revelation, like the gospels themselves, can be understood only against the actual historical and political situation of the times.[18] It is not a book of fantastic speculations about a distant future age; it is the authentic voice of prophecy pronouncing God's judgment upon the corrupting influence of power. As for Domitian himself, when his obsession with his own divine status and his insatiable hatred of all who opposed him had passed beyond endurance, he was assassinated by a retainer of his own household circle. The Senate found courage to applaud the deed and vilified his memory, ordering the deletion of his name from all public inscriptions. The historians Suetonius and Tacitus openly recorded the story of his enormities. The *Nero redivivus* was dead, to the relief not only of Jews and Christians but of all Romans who valued the older traditions of government. But the Church was as yet only on the threshold of the centuries of persecution.

IV

THE POLITICAL CHRIST IN HISTORY
AND TODAY

'Every good tree brings forth good fruit,' said Jesus, 'but a corrupt tree brings forth evil fruit ... By their fruits you shall know them' (Matt. 7.17-19; cf. Luke 6.43f.). The Christians of the age of the persecutions proved that they were truly branches of the Vine (John 15.5); that age was the Church's finest hour. In Dom Gregory Dix's phrase, they poured the warmth of Christian love into the cold heart of the Graeco-Roman world. The conclusive argument against the view that Jesus was a nationalist revolutionary leader is the quality of the life of those who were called by his name.[1] Two quotations will illustrate the character and the cause of the success of the Church's mission.

The practical application of charity was probably the most potent single cause of Christian success. The pagan comment 'See how these Christians love one another' (reported by Tertullian) was not irony. Christian charity expressed itself in care for the poor, for widows and orphans, in visits to brethren in prison or condemned to the living death of labour in the mines, and in social action in time of calamity like famine, earthquake, pestilence or war.

The paradox of the church was that it was a religious revolutionary movement, yet without a conscious political ideology; it aimed at the capture of society throughout all its strata, but was at the same time characteristic for its indifference to the possession of power in this world.[2]

The Church's role in every age is to be a fellowship of worship, witness and service. The Church's structure in any particular age must inevitably be largely determined by the social milieu in which its role has to be performed. Adaptation to environment is essential to the healthy evolution of an organic species. The Church's role does not change, but to be well adapted to the changing situation of each succeeding age means that the Church's structure must have changed often. In this respect the functional adaptation of the Church's structure was more conspicuously successful in the first millennium of its existence than in its second.

The persecution of the Christians during the reign of Diocletian, which is sometimes called 'the Age of the Martyrs', was brought to an end by the accession of Constantine (AD 312). The Church suddenly found itself basking in the sunshine of the imperial favour. Diocletian destroyed the Christians' meeting-houses: Constantine built splendid new churches for them. Now it was the turn of the enemies of the Church and even of such well-intentioned Christian dissidents as the Donatists to be persecuted. Constantine convened and inaugurated the Council of Nicea (325), the first Ecumenical Council of the Church. But the establishment of the Church by the State, which was to continue throughout Christendom until the eighteenth century and after, brought sad consequences as well as merciful relief: instead of a community of martyrs, confessors and faithful witnesses, the Church became a ladder of preferment for aspirants to high office in the State and for social climbers generally. The task of completing the establishment of Christianity as the official religion of the State was accomplished by the Emperor Theodosius (379-395), who made unbelief a capital offence;[3] but his decrees did not immediately have lasting effect. The Empire was disintegrating in the West, and the barbarians were pouring in. In 410 Rome, 'the Eternal City', was sacked by Alaric the Goth. The protection afforded to the Church by Constantine had lasted barely a century, and the Church had now an entirely new role to play. The scholarly Pope Leo I in 452 went out to meet Attila and his Huns and persuaded them to retire beyond the Danube; in 455 he dissuaded the Vandals from massacring the citizens after they had captured Rome. Armed only with spiritual weapons the bishops in their dioceses, the former imperial magistracies, pacified and after a manner Christianized the pagan hordes who had overrun and occupied the Western provinces of the Empire.

The almost incredible achievement of the Church after the utter collapse of Roman power was symbolized by the crowning of the Frankish King Charlemagne by the Pope on Christmas Day in AD 800 as the Holy Roman Emperor. Even so, as with all human triumphs, this papal success contained the seed of future trouble. Pope Leo III thought to assert papal authority when he placed the crown on the head of Charlemagne, who would have preferred to crown himself. Professor R. W. Southern has said that in creating an emperor the Pope created not a deputy, but a rival and even a master: the Pope's practical supremacy over his Emperor came to an end at the moment of the coronation. 'This action was the greatest mistake the medieval popes ever made in their effort to translate theory into practice.'[4] Five hundred years after the coronation of Charlemagne, Pope Boniface VIII was claiming that the power of the 'two swords', the secular as well as the spiritual, was given to St Peter, who acted directly through the agency of each succeeding pope. (How that verse about the 'two swords', Luke 22.38, has been misinterpreted before the rise of modern scholarship!) Doubtless during the earlier Middle Ages the Papacy had to accept the role of superintending the behaviour of emperors and princes, since some restraint upon the arbitrary power of rulers was essential, and nothing but spiritual restraints could have succeeded in that age. But the failure of the Council of Constance (1414-18) to discern the signs of the times – the rising consciousness of nationhood in Western Europe, the changing economic situation, the awakening of the laity and the new spirituality – meant that the Papacy itself would attempt to play a medieval role in the modern world. It also made the Reformation inevitable, and the Reformation in the countries where it occurred was accomplished by the will and power of the State. The legacy of Constantine and Theodosius is potent still today, although over large areas of the world's surface the State-established orthodoxy is not Christian but Marxist.

In modern English speech the word 'feudal' usually bears a derogatory implication. But the creation of 'the feudal system' out of the warring tribal settlements established by the invaders represents a notable achievement of the Church in bringing order out of the chaos of the Dark Ages, as also the Christianizing of the heathen barbarians constitutes a noble and heroic chapter in the record of the Church's missionary endeavour. The great legacy of the Roman Empire was the concept of law, and this basic requirement of civilization was somehow transmitted by the Church to the new society which was coming into being at the passing of the Dark Ages. Without the concept of a law to which even rulers themselves are subject, a law which they recognize but do not create, the achievement of genuine civilization is impossible. Benevolent despotism is the nearest alternative, but despotism is rarely benevolent. The supernatural sanctions wielded by the bishops and supremely by the Pope himself were necessary in an age in which men had still to learn that right must be done because it is right. (Will they ever learn it?)

Along with the transmission of the concept of equal law, the Church successfully undertook the role of midwife at the birth of a new super-tribal community which, though derived from many different racial stocks, was possessed of a genuine sense of belonging together. Despite its polyglot origins the community acquired a common language (Latin) in which nation could speak to nation. Long before its members called themselves 'Europeans' they referred to themselves simply as 'Christians', thus indicating the bond of their unity, which was *Christianitas* (Christendom).[5] It is true that medieval society was divided hierarchically into more or less fixed hereditary orders: nobility, freemen and serfs. But each order respected the responsibilities and restrictions of its position. Serfdom was even sometimes voluntarily accepted as a mark of service in the company of Christ the Servant of all; it was agreed that labour was a dignity bestowed upon those who were born serfs or opted to become serfs (often because of economic necessity, but sometimes chosen in the same way as entering a monastic order was chosen[6]). The dignity of labour, a biblical notion completely foreign to Graeco-Roman civilization, was a commonplace of religious instruction. It is more accurate to say that medieval Christendom did not reinstitute the ancient form of slavery than that it abolished slavery. The condition of the serfs was ameliorated by the teaching that every Christian, whatever his status, was a brother for whom Christ died.

The creation of the high civilization of the Middle Ages was an outstanding triumph of the human spirit. It was a free society in which merchants, scholars and craftsmen could move without restriction of national frontiers; where the great monastic orders could spread from one end of Christendom to the other in a shared fellowship of worship and service to the community; where the Guilds enjoyed the opportunities of free trade and a vast common market; where the university idea and its humane tradition were established and the foundations of modern science were laid. We all too easily forget that Copernicus, Kepler and Galileo stood on the shoulders of medieval man and did not spring full-grown at the threshold of the 'modern' period. Society was indeed hierarchical, but it was nevertheless 'a commonwealth in which no man was a foreigner'. Philosophy, science, art and architecture, though distinctively 'national', were yet essentially at home in every part of Christendom. Over this hierarchical commonwealth of kindreds the Pope presided at the apex; he had the advantage over emperors and princes that, whereas they and their dynasties died or failed, he, the *persona* of St Peter, endured. But every political arrangement, however admirably it has served its age, becomes obsolete in spite of, or perhaps because of, its excellence. It then restricts the free development of the human spirit. It was a far cry from the time when Pope Gregory VII (Hildebrand) on his accession (1073) wrote to 'the nations' to remind them that from the days of St Peter the see of Rome had been their Lord and Master to the years after the Great Schism of the Papacy when the Council of Constance failed in the all-important task of *aggiornamento*, the bringing up to date of the Church's structure in the light of her changing role in a new age.

From Medieval to Modern

By the sixteenth century the new awareness of their identity was well developed amongst the different 'nations' of Western Europe. Latin was giving way to the vernacular languages and dialects; 'Christendom' was being replaced by 'Europe'; Spaniards, Frenchmen, Dutchmen and Englishmen were fighting one another in the Americas for the spoils of possession. The world was enlarged, and it inevitably became a different place from the besieged fortress of Christendom, only a short while ago encircled from Vienna through the Balkans to the Levant, along the shores of Africa and round to Spain, by the armed might of Islam. Moreover, churchmen were no longer the only educated persons to whom a ruler might turn;

there was now available a new type of lay politician who proved himself useful in the service of the ruler and the nation. Liberated from tutelage to the Pope and his legates and bishops, the ruler could arrange his affairs in a manner suited to his own and his region's interests. It is significant that Luther's three famous reforming writings of 1520 were addressed to the German princes; the Reformation in the countries where it succeeded was accomplished (not only in England) by acts of State. It is not always remembered that the Thirty-nine Articles of the Church of England were written not by ecclesiastics attempting a final formulation of dogma but by statesmen anxious to reconcile extremists by means of a comprehensive, peace-seeking formula. But, of course, lay politicians were well versed in theological matters, since these were highly explosive issues which could endanger the security of the State in the days when Philip of Spain was stockpiling an armada of men-of-war in Cadiz bay. The Tudor age was a new age of the martyrs, but now Christians were martyred not by a persecuting pagan emperor but by Catholics and Protestants in the name of Christ. The legacy of Constantine and Theodosius had proved itself to be indeed a *hereditas damnosa*. In the Stewart period the Civil War ensured that in England no monarch would ever again be able to govern without the consent of Parliament, and the Commonwealth demonstrated that no government could continue indefinitely in office without the approval of the majority of the citizens. Charles and Cromwell in their different ways believed implicitly that religious unity was essential to the well-being and good government of a nation; but the doctrine was gradually abandoned after the failure of the Savoy Conference (1661) to agree upon the correct forms of ecclesiastical polity and corporate worship. The age of toleration was at hand. Theologically (or abstractly) Charles and Cromwell were right; there can be only one Church of Jesus Christ in a nation, for Christ is not divided. Politically, however, when men are in radical disagreement, government must be carried on, and the theologically correct must give way to the politically expedient. As Lord Butler has recently reminded us, politics is the art of the possible.

The age of toleration corresponds with the period often called the Enlightenment or the Age of Reason (roughly 1650-1780). Progress in the natural sciences had encouraged men to believe that the control of human nature could be achieved by the application of reason in human affairs in the same way as man's control over natural processes had been signally increased by the patient investigation of the rational laws by which the universe was ordered. Even Christianity itself must be reasonable, as John Locke argued; then controversy would cease and irrational denominational prejudices would die away. In such a climate of opinion the politician came into his own, because the area of the possible was now less constricted than in the days of autocracy. A politician must of necessity be a reasonable man. As the late President Harry Truman of the United States once remarked, a successful politician is a man who has learnt how to get on with all sorts of people, to understand their situation and their point of view, and thus to persuade and guide them. (Mr Truman also pointed out that a politician does not become a statesman until after he is dead.) He is a master of the art of showing people how they can live together despite their prejudices and interests. Politics is the art of give and take; the essence of politics is compromise, and compromise is the golden mean between extreme opinions. In a reasonable age the politician's task is to convince the minority that the will of the majority must prevail and to persuade the majority to respect the rights and opinions of the minority. Stated in this way the path of the politician sounds smooth enough, and so it would be if the Enlightenment's estimate of the essential reasonableness of human nature had not been a too optimistic simplification of the ambiguities of the human condition. The gentlemanly Whig and Tory politicians hardly noticed the growth of a vast industrial proletariat which would one day reach out its hands towards the levers of power.

Politics and the Struggle for Power

The glory and shame of the human condition is that men and nations, unlike the sun and moon and stars of light, do not automatically obey 'laws which never shall be broken' made by the Author of nature for their guidance. No sociological genius can plot the course of human behaviour as Newton was able with mathematical precision to plot the course of the heavens. Moral laws are *there*, and since before the days of Confucius or the Stoics there has been a general consensus about what they are; but men have usually chosen to disobey them when they can gain advantage for themselves by doing so. They then usually invent more or less elaborate convenience philosophies to excuse their behaviour; these rationalizations are properly known as ideologies. All individuals in greater or less measure find the exercise of power over others or in society distinctly enjoyable; they become important and have easier access to sources of wealth. Indeed, it is hard to differentiate between the love of power and the love of money, because the two are so inextricably bound up together: the one is a means to the other. Both power and wealth are sources of satisfaction which provide for many individuals their chief aim in life. A recent cartoon in *Punch* depicts a prosperous tycoon sitting in the back of his limousine saying to his schoolboy son, 'Remember this, my son: power corrupts, and absolute power is even nicer.' Though the spectacular gratification of the power-complex is given only to a few, the desire to dominate others is ingredient in all human beings from cradle to grave. This is the meaning of the Christian doctrine of original sin: we were born with this defect. 'I' identify my own desires with the moral order as such; what is right is what is good for me. I am willingly deceived by the serpent's lie: 'You shall be as God, knowing (that is in biblical language, determining) good and evil' (Gen. 3.5). I usurp the place at the centre of the universe which properly belongs to God.

Ideology is the rationalization of the serpent's lie on the collective scale: it is the identification of the interests of class, trade, profession, nation or race with the universal good, or with the moral order as such. Original sin is not an abstract dogma invented by theologians but a verifiable empirical judgment concerning the human condition. The Bible takes a realistic view of human nature. Jeremiah, that clear-sighted observer of the behaviour of politicians caught up in a desperate situation, sums up the human predicament: 'The heart is deceitful above all things and it is desperately sick; who can know it?' (17.9). The group ideologically rationalizes its own interests and identifies them with the universal good. Ideology is not rationally thought-out philosophy, though every ideological interest will have its own propagandists adopting the role of impartial 'intellectuals' and sociological pundits. They correspond to the false prophets and soothsayers of the Bible (cf. Jer. 5.1-4; 7.4). Men who in their private lives are morally responsible beings, kind to their dependents, supporters of charity, pillars of respectability in their church and neighbourhood, will nevertheless accept without criticism the ideological assumptions of their race, nation, class and social group.[7] The white man knows what is best for Africans, and it turns out that what is best for Africans is what serves the white man's interests very well: even the less than one per cent of the Gross National Product for the Third World must be made to grease the wheels of industry in the industrialized donor nation. 'The solidarity of the working class' is a maxim which suits only some of the workers some of the time: 'What's good for General Motors is good for the USA' is a slogan not only for capitalists but also for workers in industries vital to the prosperity of an exporting industrial nation. Blue-collar workers with middle-class aspirations, we read, voted in 1972 for Nixon, not for McGovern. Trade unions did not come into existence to advance the national interest; their leaders were elected as the men best qualified to obtain higher wages and better conditions for the members of a particular union. Engineering unions, for example, do not threaten to disrupt the life of the nation in order to obtain better pay for nurses. If the role which trade unions are called upon to play in the 1970s is very different from the fighting role for which their structure was created before 1939, we have here a secular instance of the difficulty of adapting an obsolescent structure to a new role, that of co-operating with government and with their hereditary class enemies, the captains of industry. On the success of this kind of adaptation, many would say, depends the survival of parliamentary democracy. If, however, government is weak and labour and capital conspire together to form an unholy alliance to exploit the consumer (while, of course, doing obeisance to the popular idol of demagogues, the housewife), the last state of the underpaid, the pensioners, the aged, the poor and the unhoused will be worse that their present unhappy condition. Only strong government, willing to undertake the task, can control the powerful interests which force up land values and create office-blocks but not homes. But where is wisdom to be found, and what is the price of understanding? Small wonder that the idealistic young are driven to proclaim the necessity of destroying 'the obscene structures of society' and to call themselves revolutionaries, but where can they turn? The Marxist proletarian revolution led to the withering away not of the State but of the individual as a person having rights over against the State. Marxist Utopianism proved to be a dangerous illusion; will the Maoist Utopianism of the polychrome 'New Left' prove to be anything more than a harmless diversion for those who cannot understand or face the harsh political realities which threaten to bring the Western achievement of parliamentary democracy to a squalid end?

Everyone knows, or ought to know by now, that the consequence of the struggle of the various power-groups in society for a larger share of the national income is inflation. Inflation has destroyed more democracies than have revolutions. The leading westernized industrial nations (with which Japan may be classified) are in the grip of inflation. They pay themselves more in dividends, salaries and wages than is justified by the output of their labour. Those who are powerful enough to do so demand and obtain increased incomes in order to keep up with the rising cost of living. Hence while the privileged members of the power-groups have (in a famous phrase) 'never had it so good', the underpaid, the unemployed, the pensioners, the aged and the poor can pick up only the crumbs which fall from the rich man's table. The 'have-nots' in our society are given the 'left-overs' after the demands of the 'haves' have been met. And this is 'charity' in the debased modern meaning of the word (cf. the slogan of the Hunger Marchers of the 1930s: 'Jarrow wants justice, not charity'). Charity in this debased sense is not a virtue; it is guilt-money paid to assuage an uneasy conscience. The point of Jesus' parable of Dives and Lazarus is usually missed (Luke 16.19-31); it does not purport to give information about the future life but aims at confronting us with our moral responsibilities in this life. The rich man was not a heartless monster who cared not at all for Lazarus, full of sores, at his gate. On the contrary, he was a decent chap, like you and me, who would not see a beggar starve. He sent his servants after the *al fresco* banquet in the courtyard to carry the left-overs to Lazarus, who was daily waiting for them at the gate on the road. Jesus did not consider 'charity' to be the fulfilment of the law of love (cf. Mark 10.17-31). Love is concerned with justice, not with 'charity'. In modern terms it is not enough for Christians to assuage their conscience by sending what they can spare to Christian Aid or Shelter or Help the Aged. In the days of Jesus political action was not a possible option for the followers of the Master, but it is possible in ours, even though politics is essentially the attempt to regulate the struggle of the conflicting power-groups in society. If in foreign affairs diplomacy is the continuation of war by other means, in home affairs politics is the continuation of the class-war without actually shooting from

95

the barricades. But this is possible only while a sense of justice still lives amongst the contestants for power. In our days Jesus' 'new commandment' of love must necessarily involve a concern for justice.

The State exists for the sake of justice; government is a necessary ingredient in the existence of human life as such. From prehistoric times this truth has been recognized; it was given expression in the age-old mythology of the king as god, or as a manifestation of the god. Even after the Hebrews had demythologized this sacred lore and stood the myth on its head, asserting that God is King, they expressed their belief in the divine institution of government: until God gave Israel a king (Saul), every man did that which was right in his own eyes (Judg. 17.6; 21.25); lawlessness, so the compiler of Judges supposed, was brought to an end by the merciful providence of God. God himself was King of Israel, and the kings of Israel or the high priests of the Jews were his vice-gerents, subject to his law of righteousness (justice). In Plato's ideal republic justice (a better translation would be 'righteousness') is the result of the harmonious working together of the three parts of human nature, whether in the individual or society: wisdom is the virtue of the rulers, courage of the soldiers, and moderation (self-control) of the lower classes of workers and citizens in general. Righteousness is the highest good and it emerges only when the individual man or the corporate State is functioning in accord with the natural harmony of the world-order.

Paul articulates the wisdom of the ancients in his profoundly Christian teaching about the State as belonging to the providential ordering of the world by God. He is a Jew converted to Christ, a Roman citizen by birth and personally aware of the benefits of the Roman administrative and legal system. Whereas nationalistic Jews might have claimed that the Jewish theocracy was the sole authority established by God, Paul with his wider experience of the world outside Palestine recognizes that God has not left the Gentiles in ignorance of the moral law, and that, even though they do not possess the Torah of Moses, they nevertheless do by nature the things of the law written upon their hearts, which operates through their conscience (Rom. 2.14f.). Later in the same epistle this evaluation of the Gentile awareness of the moral law is applied to the doctrine of the State. The *locus classicus* for the Christian doctrine of the State is to be found in Rom. 13.1-7.

Every person, says Paul, must be obedient to the 'higher powers', by which he means the duly constituted political authorities. He was writing probably about AD 57-58, perhaps from Corinth, and he must have known all about the crimes and follies of Nero, who was Emperor at the time. But he was not thinking about Nero, but about the company of hard-working and conscientious senators, administrators, provincial governors, military personnel and local magistrates, who despite their occasional lapses managed the complicated processes of government throughout the vast *imperium* of Rome. Paul then says that 'there is no power but from God': that is, all political authority derives its title to rule from God. The office of the ruler is held in trust from God, but of course heathen rulers do not know this, or know it only indirectly in so far as they are aware of the authority of conscience, that is, the obligation which they feel themselves to be under to do that which they know to be just. When Paul says that all political power is from God, he is teaching that God in his wisdom has so ordered the world that government shall provide a permanent restraint upon human selfishness; there must always be rulers and ruled. The State, that is to say, is part of the natural order (as Stoic philosophy and Catholic theology put it) or one of the Orders of Creation (in the language of Protestant theology). 'Therefore,' Paul continues, 'he who resists authority' – that is, the duly constituted political government – 'withstands the ordinance of God.' To our mind this may seem a somewhat extreme statement, but it represents the wisdom of the ancient world, where thoughtful men realized that the forces of violence lay so near to the surface of civilized life that an eruption might suddenly create havoc unless the authority of government was upheld by a law-abiding majority. Plato records how Socrates drank the hemlock, refusing to escape from prison because he would not disobey the unjust sentence passed upon him by the legitimate authority of the Athenian jury (*Crito*, 50f.). The general standpoint of the Bible is that men are naturally selfish and that without the threat of coercion and retribution civilized life would be destroyed by the unrestrained greed and callousness of the human species.

The melancholy history of the twentieth century has done nothing to qualify the doctrine of original sin. In the Lutheran phrase, the

State is a dyke against sin; it is a part of the design of a beneficent providence which preserves fallen men from the worst consequences of their own in-built destructive mechanisms. Without strong government human life would be – as Thomas Hobbes and the biblical realists agree – 'solitary, poor, nasty, brutish and short'. Weak government is a contradiction in terms, since a nominal government without the will to govern is not a government at all. An aphorism of Archbishop William Temple expresses the matter forcefully: 'It is desirable that government should be just; it is essential that it should be strong.' No Christian realist would be so foolish as to transpose the adjectives 'just' and 'strong' in this pronouncement. A weak government is a people's worst affliction. Paul stresses that the *raison d'être* of the State is to use its power for the promotion of the good and the discouragement of evil: 'He does not bear the sword in vain, for he is a minister of God (*theou diakonos*), an avenger of wrath to one who does evil.' Even a repressive and perhaps corrupt government plays an essential role in preserving the elementary decencies without which society would perish; indeed, some might think that totalitarian governments today perform this role more effectively than governments of the Western democratic type, enforcing the full rigours of the law against such anti-social offences as murder, robbery, mugging, assault, embezzlement, drunkenness, drug-pushing and the rest of the 'routine' social crimes. Many tyrannical governments remain in power because the majority of the people prefer strong-arm government to the disorder which prevails when government is weak. By modern standards the Roman administration of law was stern and its penalties were severe, but Paul was able to say, 'If you want to be free from fear of the political authority, do that which is good and you will receive commendation from it.' Rulers are not a terror to those who keep the laws but to law-breakers.

In describing the ruler as a minister (deacon) of God Paul is saying that he is performing, not indeed God's proper work of redemption, but his 'strange work' of maintaining an order of preservation in which God's purpose of redemption can go forward. Paul's use of the word *deacon* is significant because of its associations with the language of the Church's ministry and of Christ himself. There was already in existence in Paul's day an order of deacons in the Church alongside that of the bishops (cf. Phil. 1.1). The Christian tradition testifies that Jesus himself had chosen as his title

98

'the deacon' (Luke 22.27, literally 'I am in your midst as the deacon'
– the serving man; cf. Mark 10.45, 'The Son of Man came not to
be deaconed unto but to deacon') and that he had given a striking
demonstration of this teaching by washing the disciples' feet (John
13.1-11). Hence when Paul speaks of the ruler as 'a deacon of God
to thee for good', if one does well, but as 'a deacon of God, an
avenger for wrath to him that does evil', it can hardly be doubted
that he thinks of the administrators and magistrates as those who
are empowered to act as God's executives in the work of maintaining
public order and equal justice. Even more striking is the word he
uses in v. 6, where he speaks of the authorities as 'ministers of
God's service'; here the word is *leitourgoi* (cf. the English word
'liturgy') which in both classical and biblical Greek has religious
overtones, denoting the priestly offering of sacrifice. (In secular
Greek the word is also used of public benefactors, such as the rich
men who had built the baths or the stadia for their city.) Here
the service of the priesthood which offers up to God in sacrifice
the gifts of the worshippers is likely to be in Paul's mind; in Rom.
15.16 he speaks of himself as 'ministering in sacrifice the gospel of
God, that the offering up of the Gentiles might be made acceptable'
(RV margin; the NEB speaks here of Paul's priestly service as the
preaching of the gospel and his offering of the Gentiles as an acceptable sacrifice; but at 13.4 it feebly renders *diakonoi* by the colourless
word 'agents', which fails to convey the religious overtones, and at
13.7 contents itself with 'The authorities are in God's service'). The
minimum intention of Paul's use of *leitourgoi* must be that the
work of the rulers is as truly an offering to God as is the service
of the priesthood of the believers for whom he is writing. 'Liturgy'
became the regular word in the usage of the Church for the offering
to God of its worship and service, especially in the Eucharist.

THE SOURCE OF POLITICAL AUTHORITY

The teaching of the Bible as a whole and of Paul in particular stands
at the opposite pole from the eighteenth-century doctrine that
political authority is derived from the people. According to some
historians of modern thought a direct line may be traced from
Rousseau's notions of 'the general will' and 'the sovereignty of
the people' to the political messianism of Marxism or its variant

in Nazi ideology.[8] Obviously 'the people' cannot govern collectively; hence after 'the revolution', whether bloody or treacherous, 'the party' claims to represent them so completely that they need no vote, except perhaps a token vote for a list of candidates nominated by the men who have seized power. After a 'night of the long knives' or perhaps a protracted period of in-fighting within the party, a Stalin or a Hitler emerges and plays the part of a god, demythologized, of course, as befits an atheist regime. The individual is stripped of all his rights, including his right to criticize or to vote against his rulers and their policies. He is in respect of human rights worse off than the citizens of the Roman Empire, because though a play-boy like Nero or a fanatic like Domitian might be Caesar, government was carried on by administrators and magistrates who for the most part believed in the old civic virtues and in the Stoic conception of a natural law which took cognizance of the individual's claim to justice. Christian civilization, whatever its imperfections, baptized the virtues of Greek and Roman political wisdom into the service of Christ, or at least aimed at doing so. This, in fact, is what Paul was doing in Romans 12 and 13. He was investing the Roman administration of justice with its due respect as a part of the providential ordering of the world by God.

It is sometimes said that Paul inculcates an attitude of subservience to the State. This is not his intention. In his own work as the Apostle of the Gentiles he had found the Roman administration a help rather than a hindrance, as we have noted. He was writing some years before Nero's persecution and before he had gone up to Jerusalem for the last time; there he had confidence to appeal to Caesar's justice when he was in danger. If I Tim. 4.6f. ('I am already being offered-in-sacrifice and the time of my departure is come; I have fought the good fight ...') is a genuine fragment from one of his last letters, written from prison in Rome, it must be assumed that, like Socrates, he died as he had taught and lived, obediently to the laws of the duly constituted political authority. That, at least, is what the Church believed about him at a time when personal memories were still alive. He had been protected by the State and benefited from its laws; he would not renounce his teaching that the State wielded the authority given to it by God.

At this point we should note very carefully what Paul says and what he does not say. He says that the authority (power, *exousia*, Rom. 13.1) of the State is ordained or constituted by God; this is why the subjects of the State must obey the legal enactments of the State, even when it is against their personal interests to do so, and even when they personally consider that the State's verdicts against themselves are unjust. He does *not* say that the State has been endowed with a divine infallibility in its judgments in particular cases; he knows very well that all men are liable to err and that justice can and does miscarry. He does not in any way adumbrate or give consent to the doctrine of the omicompetent State, which automatically makes a decision or verdict right by the mere fact that it has enacted it. The power committed to the State by God is to reward those who do well and to punish evildoers, but this power can be and is misused by fallible rulers. Secondly, and this is a point upon which Paul is frequently misrepresented, while he says that the officers of the State collectively exercise a God-appointed authority, he does *not* say that any particular individual, whether Caesar, senator, administrator or magistrate, was personally appointed to his office by God. God did not appoint Nero (or Mr Gladstone or Stalin) to the office which he held: the free working of human political and social forces did that, whatever view Paul might have taken about the providential control of the operations of those mysterious processes. The dignity of the office must not be confused with the worthiness of the individual holder of it, as Paul must have realized with some embarrassment on the occasion recorded in Acts 23.1-5.

Paul's teaching about the duty of Christians towards the State has a timeless relevance to the political situation of every age, even though in his own day Western-democratic universal franchise was quite inconceivable. The truth is that all societies need government and its laws because of the defect of human nature, just as a lame man needs crutches. William Temple once said that he thought he would be honest enough to buy a railway-ticket for his journey, but it was the knowledge that there would be a ticket-collector at the barrier which just clinched the matter. Firm government is a necessity of human life because we are all moral weaklings; it is easy to think of more testing cases than the one in Temple's illustration. Only an extreme Utopian could convince himself that anarchism would be a feasible solution of the problem of order in society, if by anarchism is meant the abolition of government and allowing every man to do that which is right in his own eyes. Anarchism in this sense has never existed in human society, although anarchy, the disorder arising from the lack of firm government, is all too easily a possibility. The distinction between the two words is important. Paul was clearly no anarchist either in political theory or in the sense of one who incites to disorder in the State. Christians must obey the government not only from fear of punishment ('wrath') but also for conscience' sake. They should pay their taxes and give their respect to the authorities to whom honour is due.

Of course, Paul's instruction was addressed to a particular situation in time and place: the situation of small house-churches in the cities of the Roman Empire. The insights which it contains must be rethought in relation to the milieu of Christians living in social and political conditions which in many respects are vastly different. Luther found in his teaching an assurance of the rights of the local prince as over against the political claims of the Papacy, and if Lutheranism in its homeland acquired a certain reputation for subservience to the State in Bismarck's Prussia and elsewhere, it should be remembered also that the resistance to Nazi totalitarianism by the Confessing Church of Niemöller, Bonhoeffer and Count von Stauffenberg has wiped the slate clean. Albert Einstein's testimony is eloquent:

> Only the churches stood squarely across the path of Hitler's campaign for suppressing truth. I never had any special interest in the Church before, but now I feel a great affection and admiration because the Church alone has had the courage and persistence to stand for truth and moral freedom. I am forced to confess that what I once despised I now praise unreservedly.

CHRISTIANITY AND DEMOCRACY

Democracy means government by the people. The Greeks used the word to denote the direct rule of the free citizens in the assembly of the city-state; there were, of course, a lot of second- and third-class citizens with no voting rights. The democratic assembly appointed the executives who carried on the day-to-day administration; it met in full strength when popular passions ran high. Thus, a small majority of the five hundred or so members of the assembly who were present at the trial of Socrates condemned him to death. Small wonder that Plato condemned 'democracy' as a form of government; he said it was as if all the passengers on a ship claimed the right to steer and, knowing nothing about the science of navigation, ran inevitably into disaster (*Republic*, 488). An interesting example of Greek-style democracy will be found in Acts 19.23-41, the case of Demetrius v. Alexander, which arose out of Paul's denigration of Diana of the Ephesians. The mob in the open-air theatre was quietened by the town clerk; but by this date (as he pointed out) the Roman law courts were open and the proconsuls would adopt an unfavourable view of the matter if the democratic assembly took the law into their own hands. The Greek experiment of city-state democracy was short-lived, because imperial powers were arising which put an end to the independent cities as the units of government. In fact, though Aristotle did not notice the development, it was his own pupil Alexander the Great whose empire abolished the independence of the cities, which had previously combined with one another only in times of mutual danger. Nevertheless the Greek ideal of public participation in government remained as an affirmation of the inalienable rights of the people to participate in decisions concerning their own well-being and destiny.

It would be anachronistic to suppose that democratic government in our modern sense of the term could have been viable during the first millennium and a half of the Church's existence. There is no divinely revealed blueprint of the perfect political system, valid for every age, in the Bible or anywhere else. Christians must learn God's will in their own age by doing it in the midst of their own historical situation (cf. John 7.17). In the circumstances of their day Aquinas and Calvin could hardly be anything other than constitutional authoritarians. In England the word 'democratic' was long out of favour because of its use by the French revolutionaries after 1789 (and perhaps because of the exaltation of democracy in the former American colonies after the War of Independence). Nevertheless the political thought of Christians like John Locke had prepared the way for the style of constitutional government, based on an ever-widening franchise, which is the British form of democracy today. The Church from the beginning had asserted the value of every individual person or child on the basis of the Master's teaching concerning the God who cares even for the sparrows ('Are you not of much more value than they?' Matt. 6.26) and the little children (Matt. 18.10,14; Mark 9.36f.), and Christian concern could join forces with 'enlightened' humanistic opinion in working towards the type of parliamentary democracy which was established in the nineteenth century. There is no one 'ideal' form of democratic government. The forms which the democratic systems of Britain, France, West Germany, Scandinavia and the United States of America have assumed are all markedly different from one another; but they all enshrine in their own ways the basic principle of respect for the individual and for the minorities in their midst. They all doubtless assume that their particular democratic structure is best, and so it is for them, since they all have different histories; particular constitutional forms grow out of history and not out of books about political theory. The much respected and utterly impractical *Republic* of Plato is a monument to the truth of this statement. Standing in stark contrast to the Western types of democracy is the totalitarian form of autocracy which is represented by the tautologism 'People's Democracy', which means government of the people by the Party for the Party, the rule of the few over the many. The Greeks had a word for it, namely, oligarchy.

Most Christian people will probably prefer parliamentary democracy, that is, government through representatives elected by the people, to any other form of rule. It permits the acknowledgment of the sovereignty of God over the State by making room for the recognition that it is a divine responsibility with which the rulers, fallible though they are, have been entrusted: the government does not create right and wrong, but recognizes their givenness. At its best it allows for the representation of the main types of opinion amongst the population in proportion to their numerical strength. It respects minority interests and safeguards the freedom of the individual conscience. But beyond all these virtues it deals more effectively than any other political system can with the all-pervasive defect of human nature, its inbuilt selfishness, by imposing limits upon the wielders of power in the State. The rulers are ultimately answerable to the electorate which at the constitutionally appointed time can summon them to render an account of their stewardship and dismiss them if they have disappointed the hope which was placed in them. As Dr Johnson remarked, when a man knows that he is to be hanged in a fortnight, it concentrates his mind wonderfully. The accountability of rulers to the electorate, irrespectively of whether they regard themselves as responsible to God, is a principal merit of constitutional democracy. This is not a peculiarly Christian insight but a deeply human recognition. But, as Dietrich Bonhoeffer insisted, to be truly Christian is, after all, not to be different from humanity in general but to be most truly human. The Christian political ideal is not other than the human political aspiration as such. There is no such thing as a Christian political system, a truth which should not be obscured for us by the existence of so-called 'Christian' political parties in some European countries. And, since being a Christian is not to be distinguished from being truly human, there is nothing to be gained for Christ's political ministry in the world today by setting up a 'Christian' political party in rivalry to other parties. Christians engaged actively in local or national political activity should work for the common good (even if they have stood – or in America run – as Independent candidates) in co-operation with all who will work with them in promoting the policies which seem to them to be right in a particular situation.

It can reasonably be argued that representative democracy is the fairest system of government ever devised by the wit of man. The State owes its existence to the fact that the control of power is a pre-condition of civilization; in another epigram of William Temple's, 'Force is entrusted to the State in order that the State might prevent the lawless use of force.' The right to exercise power is almost too great a responsibility for any group of sinful human beings to bear, since those who hold it are tempted to use power in the interests of their own class or social group. Indeed, the election manifestos of many candidates for Parliament unashamedly make it clear that this is what they intend to do. This is why their supporters are being invited to vote for them; both the supporters and their chosen candidates have already identified their own interests with those of 'the country' as a whole. How much better it is that the struggle should be carried on not at the barricades but in the debating chamber with all the ensuing publicity of the press and the radio. The *communis sensus* of the nation as a whole is thus alerted to the issues at stake. A politically educated electorate is essential to the efficient working of parliamentary democracy, which is a delicate plant that grows slowly. The liberal optimism which imagined that the Westminster model of government could be transplanted to the former British colonies has been disappointed, as one new constitutional government after another has followed the familiar path through corruption and revolution to one-party rule. The toppled statue of 'Nkrumah, which stood before the parliamentary building in Accra bearing the inscription 'Seek ye first the political kingdom', is a warning against unrealistic estimates of human nature. It has yet to be shown that representative democracy can take root in a country which has had no tradition of Christian belief and practice or that it can survive in a nation which has lost its traditional Christian belief. Perhaps India will provide a test case for the former experiment and Britain for the latter.

CHRISTIANS IN POLITICS

Romans 13.1-7 has had a more profound influence upon the development of the political institutions of Western Europe, the former 'Christendom', than any other writing. It should, of course, be read in its context of chapters 12 and 13 and indeed of the whole New Testament. From Europe the impact of the political Christ was carried to the New World and to a considerable part of what is nowadays called the Third World. And this is all the more remarkable because Jesus was an Asian Jew who lived far from the centre of political power on the fringe of the Roman Empire. Yet the title by which he chose to define his own role in the world is still the proud title borne by the principal officers of government in many countries of the world. We still speak of a Prime Minister, Cabinet Ministers, and Ministers of many kinds, even Ministers of Posts and Telegraphs. Our political vocabulary should remind us of the rock from which we were hewn, but how many people today are conscious of its historical significance? Secularism is a forgetting of history, and in a secular climate we pass without noticing into secular phraseology, using colourless terms like 'Department of Education and Science', as though Government itself were some kind of Super Department Store. We still continue speaking of civil servants, public service, the Health Service and the like, though we have forgotten why.

The reason why, of course, is the impact of the political Christ upon the development of human institutions. Though himself acquainted with political authority only in the form of the oriental despotism of the Herods and the cold and distant military government of the occupying power, he nevertheless offered a political judgment which has exercised a more lasting influence upon the development of standards of political behaviour than have the writings of any political philosopher. 'You know that the rulers of the

106

pagan nations lord it over them and their great men domineer over them. But it shall not be so among you. Whoever would become great among you shall be your serving man, and whoever would be first among you shall be everyone's slave, even as the Son of Man came not to be served but to serve and to give his life a ransom for many' (Mark 10.43-45). Jesus identifies ruling with serving, greatness with self-offering. Paul sees the office even of the Roman political authorities as a ministry in the divine economy of preservation and their work as a divine liturgy. In modern times an impressive list could be compiled of political leaders who have found in the service of their country or of mankind the fulfilment of their vocation to the service of God.

The Christian engaged in political activity, whether at the national or local level, will view his work as the service of God through the service of mankind. He will be humble and not count his Christian profession as conferring upon him superior political expertise. The politician is professionally committed to self-justification and to the assertion of the righteousness of his party's policies: he and his party must be shown to stand for the good of the people at large. The temptation to self-righteousness is endemic, not only amongst politicians; but Jesus and Paul regard self-righteousness ('boasting') as deadly sin. Its opposite is humility, the readiness to believe in the sincerity of one's opponents and to admit the possibility that they might have some right on their side. Being willing to learn from one's opponents and to admit that one might be mistaken is one of the most difficult Christian virtues, even for those who regularly make confession of their sins. It was said of John Newton, the converted slave-trader and hymn-writer, that he confessed several times a day that he was a miserable sinner but would never admit that he was mistaken. Though the politician is professionally concerned to discredit his opponents, he must at the same time, if he is a Christian, learn to respect them and to co-operate with them in all matters on which agreement is possible. Negatively this involves a refusal to take part in those scenes of mass-hysteria in which the opposing parties scream abuse at each other across the floor of the House. Positively it involves seeking common ground with members of other parties, since parliamentary democracy can exist only so long as there is basic agreement on the rules of the game. For example, the British Labour Party rightly discouraged the opponents of the hated Industrial Relations Acts from attempting to compel its repeal by refusing to obey the courts whose duty is impartially to enforce the law. Respect for the law is an essential part of the common ground on which the political parties must stand, if parliamentary democracy is to survive.

But there is also, alas, ground common to the major political parties on which the Christian conscience might well feel that they ought not to be standing. Perhaps Christians in the different parties might get together to raise such issues, even though the reforms which they might eventually effect could take as long as it formerly took to abolish slavery. An example of this kind of issue would be the trade in arms. The peace-loving, wealthy industrialized nations of the West (with the Soviet Union) do lucrative business in selling military hardware to the warlike, impoverished non-industrial nations of the Third World, whose undernourished populations cannot afford it. Half the military aircraft of the world are powered by Rolls-Royce. Could not the Christian politicians of all the parties combine to find means to offset the unemployment which would result at home if this scandal were to be phased out? Meanwhile the education of the electorate could be undertaken (in co-operation with many who might not call themselves Christian) to create an informed public opinion which the government of the day would have to respect. Or again a campaign could be promoted both inside and outside Parliament, as indeed such short-lived campaigns have already been undertaken, in respect of the percentage of the Gross National Product to be given (without strings) to the peoples of the hungry third of the world. A more difficult exercise in Christian statesmanship would be one which attempted to restrain the government of the day from exercising its power in its own interest and for its own convenience. Since no group of men willingly limits its own power, the agreement of the opposition would also have to be sought, so that it would not re-assume the powers laid down by the government, if or when it obtained an electoral majority. An example of such a reform might be of the following kind. Inflation is known to present the most serious threat to the national economy and to the continuance of democratic government itself. But one of the main causes of inflation is government spending, which may indeed be socially useful but which has the greater attraction of making the government popular with the electorate, especially before an election. The temptation to print more paper money is one which governments find hard to resist. Dr Nathaniel Micklem has urged that the management and control of the currency should be entrusted to a body comparable to the judiciary in being wholly independent of political control.[9] An all-party agreement upon such a reform, if it could be reached, would be the supreme political achievement of the twentieth century and the triumphant vindication of parliamentary democracy in the hour of its gravest danger.

CHRISTIANS AND REVOLUTION

Revolutions come in different shapes, sizes and qualities. The most likely one in Britain is the one which might occur if inflation became uncontrollable. If the strong trade unions, rejecting any form of wage-restraint, were to paralyse the economic life of the nation by strike action, the constitution could be overthrown and the militants might assume control. This, of course, is what a small but intransigent minority of revolutionary leaders are working for, the setting up of a 'people's democracy'. If the two main British parliamentary parties do not recognize the necessity of agreeing to stand together against the common enemy, the constitution could be overthrown and seven hundred years of parliamentary evolution could end ingloriously. In times of danger, such as war or industrial anarchy, it is essential that government should be strong. Sentimental memories of the days when the unions fought with fraternal concern for the weak and the exploited are out of place in an age when well-off groups of workers destroy the livelihood of their less well-placed fellow-workers by their policy of might is right. The cloth-cap image has been obliterated by the spectacle of the militant anoraks on the picket-line.

Christians will much more readily sympathize with the revolutionary attitude of many of the younger generation in many lands. It is hardly surprising that the latter, having taken a hard look at the world into which they did not ask to be born, do not like what they see. It seems to them to be a world in which the worth of the individual is reckoned in terms of his utility to the complex military-industrial machine through the operation of which the rich get richer and the poor get poorer. They do not want to be cogs in the machine, even though they might find a comfortable and well-greased slot within it. Many students do not wish to qualify for a successful career in business or in the educational sausage-machine.

Science and technology and the university itself seem to them to have become the servants of the repressive society, not the great benefactors which former generations thought they would become. Their style of life therefore represents a protest against the conventions and values of society. Politically they reject all the parties for which they have become qualified to vote, since they all (including the Labour Party) are content to do battle for the spoils of the capitalist system. Russia has betrayed the ideals of Marxism, and so they look (if anywhere) to China, Cuba and Albania as bearers of promise for the future. The philosopher of the movement is Herbert Marcuse, a German septuagenarian who produces heavily Teutonic treatises from his haven in California. He is a Marxist who would justify the overthrow of capitalist industrial society by means of revolution carried through by alienated workers, disenchanted students and oppressed racial minorities.[10] Down in the real world, however, the militant industrial workers are little concerned about oppressed minorities and chase away the demo-loving young.

Revolution as such does not fall within the scope of this book, since violent action against established authority is the abandoning of politics altogether. There are indeed situations in some parts of the world today in which a terrible decision confronts the conscience of Christian people. One can only feel humble when confronted by the moving document written by seven Dominican priests and smuggled out of the Sao Paulo prison in Brazil.[11] It is not for us to judge those priests who in a desperate situation have been prepared to kill and be killed, having cast in their lot with the victims of an unjust social order. To suffer with Christ in the place where he suffers is the noblest form of ministry and witness. Even so, revolutionary romantic idealism is a particularly treacherous version of the serpent's lie, since it at the same time inspires heroic deeds of self-sacrifice and sanctions repulsive acts of terrorism. Revolution when successful has so often merely replaced one form of dictatorship by another; the liquidation of the capitalists and the bourgeoisie does not of itself ensure popular participation in the government of their country. Those who seize power can always find sufficient 'enemies of the people' to justify their retention of it. Many will think that the courageous style of Archbishop Helder Camara of Recife in north-east Brazil may in the long run prove more effective: he says fearlessly that in Latin America Christianity has been for centuries the opium of the people and that the Church has blessed an oppressive social order. But he sees that though capitalism and authentic Christianity are irreconcilable, there is no less difficulty in reconciling Christianity with the socialistic models operating in the world today. One can indeed admire the courage of those who, like the Berrigan brothers, protest against the policies of their nation, when they believe them to be wrong. But we should reflect that it is only in a country with a tradition of constitutional democracy that such protest could happen. Angela Davis was acquitted by an American court and was fêted in lands where political prisoners are not usually brought to trial.

The so-called 'theology of revolution' lacks the hard thinking needed to make it convincing. Relying on a picture of Jesus the Revolutionary which historical study does not authenticate, it frequently seeks justification for violence by its assertion that the State itself is the prime perpetrator of violence against the people and that it must therefore be met by violence. It does not distinguish between violence and force – the force which is entrusted to the State in order that the State may prevent the lawless use of force. However plausible this argument may sound in certain areas of the world, the alarming increase in all Western countries of every form of violence from hi-jacking to mugging underlines the need to distinguish between the legitimate use of force by the State and the resort to violence by self-appointed vindicators. It is doubtless true that in some politically backward countries no action other than armed revolt can bring about change, but elsewhere political initiatives are still possible. When a French priest asserts that 'there is no violence in French society except that done by the police',[12] exaggeration passes over into hysteria, a characteristic feature of mob revolution. In a complex industrial society the dangers of such talk are painfully obvious. Martin Luther King points a different way, even though in an age of violence it can lead to an assassin's bullet. Moral choices in such a world as this are never simply between good and evil; they involve costly decision about which course is the lesser evil. Probably few Christians would deny that in plotting the assassination of Hitler in July 1944 Count C. S. von Stauffenberg and his associates were choosing the lesser evil and in this sense were doing the *right* thing. Bonhoeffer, though he judged resistance right, felt himself deeply involved in human guilt through having to fight evil by evil means. But this is the situation inherent in all

political activity, because sinful men have lost the simple possibility
of doing things which are wholly right.

The Churches and Politics Today

The ever-increasing absorption of the various denominations of the
Church in their own internal affairs has coincided with the decline
of lay interest in the churches and the fall in church membership.
The revision of liturgies, or explanations of why Anglo-Catholic
and Evangelical Anglicans cannot approve a scheme of Anglican-
Methodist reunion, or of why Roman Catholics and Anglicans cannot join together in the sacrament of unity, seem as remote from
the real issues of the contemporary world as the theological disputations of the medieval schoolmen. Indeed, the word 'theological' in
the vocabulary of the Labour Party has become a pejorative expression denoting tedious disputation over long-dead issues. However,
the political Christ is not confined within the churches. New and
vigorous societies, for the most part set up by Christian leaders but
now completely free from denominational complications, have en-
listed the support of thousands of hard-working helpers in the service
of the world's poor, the unsheltered, the disabled, the aged, the
friendless of every kind: they are free to accept the help of all
people of good will, irrespective of ecclesiastical allegiance. The
political Christ will not be edged out of the world and on to a
committee; he belongs to the real world where decisions are made
and action takes place. There are doubtless many dedicated men and
women active in national or local political and social affairs who
would be surprised to hear the voice which says, 'Come, ye blessed
of my Father, inherit the kingdom prepared for you' (Matt. 25.34). It
is especially important in these days that men and women who are
conscious of their Christian vocation should regard their work as a
real ministry in God's service and as the liturgy which they offer
to Christ. For, as Dr J. H. Oldham constantly used to remind us,
the only way in which we can serve God in the world is through the
service of our fellow men.

NOTES

CHAPTER I

1. The Christ-myth theory (that Jesus never lived) had a certain vogue at the beginning of this century but is not supported by contemporary scholarship. The leading exposition of it is found in Arthur Drews, *Die Christusmythe* (2 vols., Jena 1909-11; Eng. trans. London and Leipzig 1910). It still remains official Marxist dogma.

2. C. Dawson, *Understanding Europe*, Sheed and Ward 1952, 28.

3. Philo, *ad Gaium*, 38.

4. In the second century Justin Martyr and Tertullian say that Pilate made a report to Tiberius of the trial of Jesus, but it is not likely that they had any reliable information on the subject. Tertullian also says that Pilate became a Christian; later medieval tradition assumed that his wife had convinced him of the truth of Christ's divinity (cf. Matt. 27.19, doubtless the source of this belief). In the medieval mystery plays Pilate and his wife go up the ladder to heaven, while Annas and Caiaphas disappear into the fires of hell. In the Coptic Church Pilate became a saint and in the Greek Church Pilate's wife Claudia (? II Tim. 4.21) is honoured as a saint on October 27. The verdicts of history are not irreversible.

5. Haim Cohn, *The Trial and Death of Jesus*, Weidenfeld and Nicolson 1972.

6. Cf. Joseph de Maistre, *Lettres et Opuscules Inédits*, 1811: 'Toute nation a le gouvernement qu' elle merite.'

7. Cf. La Rochefoucauld (1613-80), *Maximes* 218: 'L' hypocrisie est un hommage que le vice rend à la vertu.'

8. J. Jeremias, *New Testament Theology*, Vol. I, Eng. trans., SCM Press and Scribners 1971, (German also 1971) shows how the recorded words of Jesus in the gospels have in very many instances an authentic Palestinian–Aramaic ring which renders it incredible that they were composed outside Palestine during the process of

developing a 'community theology' in the Hellenistic environment of the missionary churches.

9. E.g. *The Merchant of Venice*, I, ii. 42.

10. On the Samaritans see M. Gaster, *The Samaritans* (Schweich Lectures for 1923), Oxford University Press 1925.

CHAPTER II

1. See W. R. Farmer, *Maccabees, Zealots and Josephus*, Oxford University Press 1956; D. R. Griffiths, *The New Testament and the Roman State*, John Penry Press, Swansea, 1970.

2. See the commentaries, e.g. J. M. Creed, *The Gospel according to St Luke*, Macmillan 1930, 28f.; A. R. C. Leaney, *A Commentary on the Gospel according to St Luke*, A. and C. Black 1958, 44ff. Luke himself (1.5) implies that Jesus was born in the days of King Herod, i.e., before 4 BC, a date which accords well with Luke 3.23 ('Jesus was about thirty years of age when he began to teach').

3. *Antiquities* XVIII, 4-10 (Loeb ed.). Josephus' *Antiquities of the Jews*, published in AD 93, recounts the history of the Jews from the earliest times until the outbreak of the Jewish War in 66; it never mentions the Zealots. His earlier work *On the Jewish War*, written at some date after 75, does not mention the Zealots until he reaches the year 66, and then the term is used of a particular group of militants, never as a general designation of resistance fighters as a whole. See Marc Borg, 'The Currency of the Term "Zealot"', *Journal of Theological Studies*, N.S., Vol. XXII, Part 2, Oct. 1971, 504-12.

4. Cf. the popular hymn by George MacDonald (1824-1905), 'They all were looking for a king'.

5. *Antiquities*, XVIII, 63.

6. See his book *Jesus* (1926), Eng. trans. *Jesus and the Word*, Fontana 1958, 48ff.

7. *Theology of the New Testament*, Eng. trans., Vol. I, SCM Press and Scribners 1952, 20, 26-32; Vol. II, 1955.

8. Ibid. I, 20.

9. In 'The Primitive Christian Kerygma and the Historical Jesus', in C. E. Braaten and R. A. Harrisville (eds.), *The Historical Jesus and the Kerygmatic Christ*, Abingdon Press, Nashville, 1964, 27.

10. Ernst Käsemann, one of Bultmann's leading disciples, in his book *Jesus Means Freedom* (Eng. trans., SCM Press 1969, of *Der Ruf*

der Freiheit, 3rd ed., Tübingen 1968), a best seller in Germany, deals chiefly with a church quarrel in Germany; it sheds little light on the subject of our enquiry. He assumes without argument that Zealots were attracted to Jesus (19,31) and says that 'Jesus converted Zealots' (134). Though Jesus was crucified 'between Zealots to show that he was being executed as a messianic insurgent against Rome', it was really the devout Jews and their theologians who were responsible for his death (28): just as the devout theologians of the German churches had been persecuting the theologians of the Bultmann school presumably! Later he says that 'it is very doubtful whether Jesus was particularly involved in the Zealot problem' (134) and he finally remarks that 'he (Jesus) himself was no Zealot' (136). It would appear that, like so many others, he uses the word 'Zealot' loosely to mean nationalist freedom-fighters, although there is no evidence that an organized Zealot faction was in existence before the outbreak of the Jewish War. To say these things is not to deny the value of Professor Käsemann's exposition of the meaning of freedom in the New Testament. We are on his side in his protest against the obscurantism which deprecates the freedom of scholarly enquiry.

11. Thus Jeremias, *New Testament Theology* I, SCM Press 1971, 279. See also D. R. Catchpole, 'The Problem of the Historicity of the Sanhedrin Trial', in *The Trial of Jesus*, ed. Ernst Bammel (Studies in Biblical Theology, Second Series 13), SCM Press and Allenson 1970, 62f.; J. E. Allen, 'Why Pilate?', in the same work, 78-83.

12. *Von Reimarus zu Wrede*, Tübingen 1906; Eng. trans., *The Quest of the Historical Jesus*, A. and C. Black 1910; 3rd ed. with new preface, 1954. Reimarus, much influenced by English deism, was a thoroughgoing rationalist, rejecting the idea of revelation altogether. He posed in a crude form the question with which New Testament scholarship has wrestled ever since his day by his claim that the real Jesus ('the Jesus of history' of the nineteenth-century 'quest') was utterly unlike the portrait of him which the apostolic Church has bequeathed to us in the New Testament: Jesus was in fact the would-be leader of a revolutionary movement. See *Reimarus: Fragments*, ed. C. H. Talbert ('Lives of Jesus' Series), 1971, esp. 144-153.

13. R. Eisler, *The Messiah Jesus and John the Baptist*, Methuen 1931; P. Winter, *On the Trial of Jesus*, de Gruyter, Berlin, 1961.

14. Käsemann's essay 'Das Problem des historischen Jesus' in *Zeitschrift für Theologie und Kirche*, 51, 1954 (Eng. trans. in *Essays*

on New Testament Themes, SBT 41, SCM Press and Allenson 1964) is generally regarded as initiating the 'new quest'.

15. Eng. trans. *Jesus of Nazareth*, Hodder and Stoughton 1960, Harper 1961, 33, 164. The first German edition was published in 1956.

16. Op. cit., 66.

17. See note 10 above.

18. Cf. Marc Borg, op. cit., 507.

19. It is interesting that Bornkamm (op. cit., 66) says that Matt. 11.12 involves 'a sharp refusal to have anything to do with the political Messianic movement of the Zealots'.

20. On this subject see Ethelbert Stauffer, *Christ and the Caesars*, Eng. trans., SCM Press and Westminster Press 1955, 112-137, where photographs of the silver denarius will be found.

21. Andrew Sinclair, *Guevara*, Fontana 1970, 88; cf. also 42.

CHAPTER III

1. E. Renan, *The Life of Jesus*, Everyman edition, 1927, 227.

2. *The Fall of Jerusalem and the Christian Church*, SPCK 1951, 2nd ed., 1957; *Jesus and the Zealots*, Manchester Univ. Press 1967.

3. *Antiquities*, XVIII, 63-4: One of the two so-called *Testimonia Flaviana* in the writings of Josephus, neither of which can be trusted because of the likelihood of tampering with the text by Christian scribes.

4. Eusebius, *Ecclesiastical History*, III, v. 2-3.

5. *The Fall of Jerusalem*, 170-2.

6. O. Cullmann in *The State in the New Testament* (SCM Press 1957) restated the view put forward fifty years earlier that 'Iscariot' is derived from *sicarius*. M. Hengel in *Die Zeloten* (Leiden 1961) disputes it on the ground that according to Josephus the *sicarii* first appeared when Felix was procurator (AD 52-60). Brandon replies that the name 'could easily have been later assigned to Judas, if he were a Zealot' (204n.). The more usually accepted view is that 'Iscariot' means 'of Kerioth'; there were two places of that name in the region.

7. M. Hengel, *Was Jesus a Revolutionist?* Fortress Press and Blackwell 1971, 19.

8. W. Wrede, *Das Messiasgeheimnis in den Evangelien*, Göttingen 1901.

9. The question of the interpretation of the New Testament in contemporary scholarly enquiry is too vast for discussion here. One illustrative quotation must suffice. It is taken from Professor C. F. D. Moule's *The Phenomenon of the New Testament* (Studies in Biblical Theology, 2. 1), SCM Press and Allenson 1967, 80f.: 'Recent theological writing has tended to dismiss the importance of history in favour of the transcendental call to decision; or, alternatively, to dismiss the transcendent in favour of such history as can be confined within the categories of purely human comprehension. But I cannot see how a serious student of Christian origins can concur with either. It seems to me to be at once the most striking and the most disquieting character of the Gospels that they steadily refuse to be settled in either direction. On the one hand, the old Liberal Protestant way of stripping off the transcendental and rendering the Gospels rationalistically intelligible is widely agreed to have proved to be a *cul de sac*; and its repetition by those who try to present Christian doctrine without transcendence has no advantage over it, as far as I can see, except a more modern sound. On the other hand, a Gospel which cares only for the apostolic proclamation and denies that it either can or should be tested for its historical antecedents, is really only a thinly veiled gnosticism or docetism and, however much it may continue to move by a borrowed momentum, will prove ultimately to be no Gospel.'

10. Cf. the last book of his *Jewish War* (VII, 268-70).

11. See, e.g., C. H. Dodd, *The Apostolic Preaching and its Development*, Hodder and Stoughton 1936.

12. We do not know precisely what connexion Peter had with the epistle which bears his name, but it is unlikely that the ancient Church would have associated the work with Peter if it had suspected that Peter had been a leader of a 'para-Zealot' sect which hoped by revolutionary action to restore the kingdom to Israel.

13. Cf. the seventh book of the Nicomachean Ethics.

14. *Was Jesus a Revolutionist?*, 14.

15. On this whole question see Oscar Cullmann, *Peter, Disciple – Apostle – Martyr*, Eng. trans., 2nd revised ed., SCM Press and Westminster Press 1962, 71-157.

16. F. C. Synge, *Philippians and Colossians*, Torch Commentaries, SCM Press and Macmillan, New York, 1951, 49.

17. For a convenient summary of the extant evidence concerning persecution in the early Church see J. Stevenson, *A New Eusebius: Documents illustrative of the history of the Church to* AD 337, SPCK

and Macmillan, New York, 1957, 2-49.

18. The well-illustrated and readable treatment of the historical and political situation in Domitian's reign in Ethelbert Stauffer's *Christ and the Caesars*, SCM Press 1955, 147-191, 'Domitian and John', has in broad outline been followed here.

CHAPTER IV

1. Cf. J. A. Baker, *The Foolishness of God*, Darton, Longman and Todd 1971, 184-7.

2. The quotations are from Henry Chadwick, *The Early Church* (Pelican History of the Church, Vol. 1), 1967, 56 and 69.

3. See N. Q. King, *The Emperor Theodosius and the Establishment of Christianity*, SCM Press and Westminster Press 1961.

4. R. W. Southern, *Western Society and the Church in the Middle Ages* (Pelican History of the Church, Vol. 2), 1970, 99.

5. Cf. Denis Hay, *Europe: the Emergence of an Idea*, Edinburgh University Press 1957, 56: 'The very existence of a vernacular noun "Christian", meaning no more (and no less) than "person", gives a vivid indication that religion rather than race or government or geography formed the common basis of all groups in Western society. To be a Christian meant full humanity in opposition to the brute beasts.' The medieval Christian thus anticipated Bonhoeffer's discovery by a thousand years.

6. Cf. R. W. Southern, *The Making of the Middle Ages* (1953), Hutchinson 1967, 96-114.

7. Reinhold Niebuhr's *Moral Man and Immoral Society* was published in New York as long ago as 1932.

8. E.g., J. L. Talmon, *The Origins of Totalitarian Democracy*, Secker and Warburg 1952, 43, 249-253.

9. In a letter to *The Times*, 25 Jan. 1973.

10. For a critical exposition see Alasdair MacIntyre, *Marcuse*, Fontana 1970.

11. See *New Blackfriars*, Nov. 1970, or the extract from it quoted in *The Times*, 20 Nov. 1970, under the title 'The Theology of Revolution'.

12. *Témoignage chrétien*, 2 Feb. 1968, quoted by Jacques Ellul in his book *Violence*, London, 1970, 124n. Ellul is a distinguished Professor of Law; his book is subtitled 'Reflections from a Christian Perspective'.